THE STRUGGLE FOR SURVIVAL

John Hanks

THE STRUGGLE FOR SURVIVAL

The elephant problem

MAYFLOWER BOOKS
NEW YORK

All rights reserved under International and Pan American Copyright
Convention. Published in the United States by Mayflower Books,
Inc., 575 Lexington Avenue, New York City 10022. Originally
published in South Africa by C. Struik Publishers, Cape Town.

Designed by Wim Reinders, Cape Town
Lithographic reproduction by Unifoto (Pty) Limited, Cape Town
Photoset by McManus Bros (Pty) Limited, Cape Town
Printed and bound by National Book Printers,
Goodwood, Cape Province

ISBN 0 8317 2756 x

Manufactured in the Republic of South Africa
First American Edition

Contents

Acknowledgements

I am indebted to many individuals and organisations for assistance and encouragement both for my elephant research in Zambia and in the preparation of this book. My original interest in elephants was stimulated at Cambridge by Dr R. V. Short, and it was at all times a privilege and pleasure to work under his guidance during my doctoral thesis. The completion of my thesis in Cambridge was made possible by a grant from the World Wildlife Fund, which is very gratefully acknowledged.

I would like to thank the following for help in various ways: Dr P. Albl, Messrs J. L. Anderson, W. F. H. Ansell, W. R. Bainbridge, J. Botha, J. Church, P. Guy, R. Langeveld, Dr W. Leuthold, Messrs P. W. Martin, R. Martin, Dr J. E. A. McIntosh, Messrs. A. Phiri, J. A. Pile, and the UN/FAO Luangwa Valley Conservation and Development Project. I would also like to thank Jane Lee for drawing Figures 5, 9 and 16, and to thank the Editors of the following journals for permission to reproduce figures and photographs: *Journal of Reproduction and Fertility* for Figure 6, 13 and 15 and Plate 32; *Arnoldia (Rhodesia)* for Figure 4; *Rhodesia Science News* for Figure 23.

The final word of thanks must go to my wife Carol for typing the manuscript and for her help and encouragement throughout my own elephant research.

CONTRIBUTING PHOTOGRAPHERS

P. Albl 54
W. R. Bainbridge 1, 2, 14, 15, 18, 68, 69, 70
A. Bannister 58
R. Cantel 9, 11, 19, 20, 53, 71
G. Cubitt 10, 16, 61, 65, 67
P. Guy 5
F. Hartmann 7, 13, 24, 45, 64, 75
J. Hanks 3, 4, 12, 22, 25, 26, 27, 28, 29, 30, 32 top, 62, 72, 73
P. Johnson 17, 21, 55, 56, 63, 66
P. Jordan 74
G. Komnick 57
W. Leuthold 31, 33, 34, 35, 36, 37, 38, 39, 40, 41, 42, 43, 44, 59
National Parks Board of Trustees 60
D. Parry 6
Rhodesia Herald 23
R. V. Short 32 (bottom)
C. Spinage 8
E. Wiedemann 46, 47, 48, 49, 50, 51, 52

Author's note

There is no doubt that the greatest single threat to the future of wildlife and wildlife habitats in the whole of Africa is the very high rate of human population growth. I came to appreciate this fact when I was studying an elephant problem in the Luangwa Valley in Zambia, and subsequently I have had confirmation of this from several other parts of the continent.

In the last decade, a spate of wildlife books has stimulated interest in the natural history of Africa as never before, but as far as I can see, the true and frightening story of the elephant problem remains untold. In this book I have tried to put the record straight. *The Elephant Problem* is based mainly on my own experiences in Zambia and Rhodesia. I have included the work of others for comparative purposes or for those parts of the book where my own observations were inadequate.

This is not intended to be a definitive work on elephants; such texts are available elsewhere. I have concentrated on those parts of elephant biology that are relevant to what I call 'the elephant problem' – feeding habits and impact on the vegetation, age determination and body growth, reproduction, mortality, and finally the determination of elephant numbers and movement patterns. Since the book is written for the general reader, I have tried to keep scientific terms to an absolute minimum. Inevitably, some must be included, and there is a glossary for those who are unfamiliar with them. The references to each chapter are found on p169 and they include the more important relevant publications for those who are interested in further reading, but I must warn that the list is not intended to be comprehensive.

Throughout this book I have used the names of countries and wildlife sanctuaries as they were when the studies were carried out. The recent name changes are at times a little confusing and for easy future reference I list them here.

NAME CHANGES

Botswana: formerly Bechuanaland
Malawi: formerly Nyasaland
Rhodesia – Zimbabwe: formerly Southern Rhodesia
Tanzania: formerly Tanganyika and Zanzibar
Zaire: formerly Belgian Congo
Zambia: formerly Northern Rhodesia
Kabalega Falls National Park: formerly Murchison Falls National Park
Rwenzori National Park: formerly Queen Elizabeth National Park
South Luangwa National Park: formerly South Luangwa Game Reserve

1
Introduction

The Smithsonian Institution Identification Manual for African Mammals recognises one species of African elephant, Loxodonta africana, *with two main divisons,* africana, *the bush elephant, and* cyclotis, *the forest elephant. Unless otherwise stated, all references in this book will be to the bush elephant.*

I have been asked many times how I became involved in elephant research. To answer this, I have to go back to a cold British winter's day in Norfolk when I was sitting in school absolutely enthralled by a book that had just been published called *Serengeti shall not die.* Subsequently of course, Grzimek's book has become a classic, but at that time his name, and the name of Serengeti, were not that well-known in Britain. I had never been to Africa, and all the places and animals he described were new to me. This excited my imagination as no book had ever done before, and I became quite determined that this was the sort of work I wanted to do. After I had gained my entrance to Cambridge I had nine months free before the University term started and I sent off letters to various people and organisations in Britain and East Africa, naively offering my services to wildlife conservation in return for a very basic salary, board and lodgings. I did not appreciate that many other people had the same idea, and I was disappointed when most of my letters went unanswered – or came back with a curt reply to the effect that I was not wanted.

The one exception, a letter I had addressed to the World Wildlife Fund in London, ended up on the desk of Ian Macphail. He appreciated my youthful enthusiasm and gave me several introductions and useful contacts in Kenya. Armed with these I set off first for Nairobi, and then, over the next six months, various parts of East Africa.

I need not recall my activities over all of this period; most of them are irrelevant to this book, but I must mention briefly the month I spent with Ian Parker on the Galana River Game Management Scheme near Tsavo National Park. Ian Parker introduced me to a very wild and beautiful part of Africa, and I accompanied him on several trips to capture and immobilise young elephants. During the days I spent with him, we had many lengthy discussions through which I came to appreciate that although the European had been hunting elephants ever since he first set foot in Africa, surprisingly little was known about any aspect of elephant biology.

My visit to East Africa, the Galana area in particular, made me determined to return to Africa as soon as I had graduated, and stimulated an interest in elephants that was further enhanced by my supervisor in Cambridge, Roger Short, who during my final year at University spent several months studying elephants in Uganda. He came back full of exciting ideas for new projects. Encouraged by his infectious enthusiasm, I made provisional plans with him to go to Uganda on graduation to study aspects of elephant reproduction.

However, it soon became clear that I was going to find it difficult to get financial support for the project, and I became rather despondent. Then, one day in May, just before my final exams, I was wrapping up rubbish in a piece of old newspaper when I noticed an advertisement for a biologist to work in the Kafue National Park in Zambia. The newspaper was only a few days old so I quickly wrote off for application forms. I was not all that sure where Zambia was, and I had certainly never heard of the Kafue National Park, but at least it was in Africa and there were bound to be elephants somewhere nearby!

Early in June I was called up to London for an interview with the Ministry of Overseas Development in one of those faceless and impersonal buildings that epitomise the Civil Service. It all seemed very remote from Africa. I cannot remember much about the interview except that two members of the interviewing board were ex-colonial service and they were both quite impressed by the fact that I had already been to Africa and wanted to return. The only other event of any significance that I can remember that day was a question that came from one of the ex-colonial gentlemen. Leaning forward, and looking me straight in the eye, he said, 'My boy, can you shoot?' My reply in the affirmative seemed to please him, and after a few more pleasantries the interview came to an end.

I returned to Cambridge where a week later I received a letter of appointment for a three-year contract, with a request that I start work as soon as possible after the first of September.

From a position of despondency and uncertainty my return to Africa was suddenly confirmed, although it appeared that an immediate project on elephants was out of the question. It was at least a step in the right direction.

In my second year at Cambridge I had met Carol, my wife-to-be, who was training as a nurse at Addenbrookes Hospital. We announced our engagement just after my letter of appointment arrived and began to make plans for our move to Africa. I scoured the local libraries for references to Kafue National Park, but besides a mention of its existence – and the fact that at over 22 400 square kilometres it is one of the largest national parks in the world – I could find very little worthwhile information.

Compared to Serengeti, Kafue seemed a nonentity to the outside world. We did not know what to expect in Zambia. I warned Carol that we would almost certainly be living on an outstation with basic housing and very limited facilities. She became very excited at the thought of the challenge and quite determined to make use of her nursing experience. We were married in August, and early in September I flew out to Zambia, Carol remaining behind for seven weeks to complete her training.

10

I arrived in Lusaka about one month before Zambia's first anniversary of Independence. In those days Zambia was at the start of a post-independence boom. There was a general atmosphere of confidence in the future, and I was surprised at the amount of development that was taking place in and around the capital. I spent my first night in a government hostel in Lusaka, and the next morning was taken out to the Headquarters of the Department of Game and Fisheries at Chilanga, about 16 kilometres from the city centre.

The building had an unmistakable 'Game Department' air about it, staffed by what I soon came to recognise as black and white stereotypes to complete the picture. I was met by Bill Bainbridge, the Chief Game Officer, and for the next two hours he sat me down and bubbled away enthusiastically about the 'elephant problem' in the Luangwa Valley. Luangwa had become his great love and, as I was to discover over the next six years, the elephants in the Luangwa and their impact on the vegetation became an all-consuming interest of his – at times almost at the expense of all his other responsibilities. In fact, during my first few days in Zambia, I found out very little about the Kafue National Park or my new job – we spent nearly all our time talking about elephants!

Early the next morning I flew with Bill down to the Luangwa Valley where I met the Warden, Johnny Uys. We went straight out into the field to look at the destruction of the woody vegetation we had talked about in Lusaka, and then moved on to watch Game Department hunters shooting and killing elephants inside the boundaries of the Game Reserve. It was all very sudden and new to me and I must admit to being quite appalled by what I saw: Was all this killing really necessary?

For the next five days I travelled around various parts of the valley with Bill who told me why he, and others, considered it necessary to kill literally hundreds of elephants inside the very areas that had been set aside to conserve the fauna and flora of the country.

To put it in very simple terms, the elephants were being killed because their prolific, extravagant and wasteful feeding habits were causing spectacular changes in the vegetation. Under the elephant's influence, enormous and stately baobabs were reduced to pulp; diverse and productive woodland converted to open grassland; and habitats modified almost beyond recognition. Bill argued that these rapid changes of the habitat were unnatural and most undesirable. He felt that elephants must be killed to control the damage, but admitted that this was not universally accepted. He recognised that others advocated a laissez-faire policy, maintaining that we should stand back, wait, and let nature take its course.

This was the basis of the controversy: two extreme points of view which made the 'elephant problem' one of the most hotly debated topics in the field of African wildlife conservation, with strong emotions often over-riding objective argument.

Unfortunately, it appeared that there was still a great deal of confusion surrounding the issue, and the managers of the reserves were being placed in an unenviable position. There was still uncertainty as to why the elephants had increased; there was also a frightening lack of hard facts and figures on the number of elephants in the area, their rate of increase and their impact on the vegetation. There was, however, no shortage of emotion-charged opinion. The decision makers, who in most cases lacked biological training, did not know what to do: should they kill the elephants, or leave it to nature? I returned to Chilanga after my short visit to Luangwa acutely aware of the enormous potential that existed in the area for an exciting research project.

My move out to Ngoma, the headquarters of the Kafue National Park, was something of an anti-climax. In 1965 there were only about 200 elephants in the whole reserve, and they were wild, unapproachable and rarely seen. Needless to say they were not considered a research priority. My brief was to prepare a vegetation map of the Park, to maintain the herbarium and to continue basic biological data collection. Although the research programme was not quite what I had hoped for, I was pleasantly surprised at the facilities available at Ngoma. A new laboratory block was being built and the herbarium was already well-established. I spent two days with Bill Mitchell, the retiring biologist, who tried to cram in as much as he could before he returned to Livingstone, and then he left me to it.

I had been given an attractive three-bedroomed house, well removed from the main camp. Ngoma itself is on a small hill overlooking the Nkala floodplain, and it is backed up by a magnificent forest of Rhodesian teak. On most days I could see waterbuck, zebra and buffalo close by. It was a most attractive setting, and I wrote to Cambridge telling Carol that her first days in Africa would not be spent living in a mud hut after all.

In addition to three other European families at Ngoma, there was a resident African population, including wives and children, of over 300. We were 170 kilometres on a dirt road from Kalomo, our nearest town, and about 16 kilometres from the Kafue River.

My first few weeks were spent getting to know the 22 400 square kilometres of the Park. I had been given an enormous task. All the plants and animals were new to me, and time seemed to flash by as I set about learning all I could about my new environment. It seemed no time at all before Carol arrived at Lusaka, having completed her final State Registration examinations that week, and after a day in the city to buy all our provisions for the next three months, we returned to Ngoma.

Carol was delighted with our new home and surroundings and was quick to settle in to a completely new way of life. Ngoma had no telephone link with the outside world. Any urgent messages to or from the station came through the Department's internal radio network from Chilanga. A few days after Carol arrived, a telegram for us came from Cambridge saying 'Congratulations on your SON'. It was read out to us on the radio (for all to hear of course) and caused great amusement, as most people knew by then that we had only been married for a couple of months. The telegram should have read 'Congratulations on your SRN', telling Carol that she had passed her final nursing examinations, but somewhere along the line somebody at Headquarters had decided that 'SRN' couldn't possibly be right, and that 'SON' would look much better! With her nursing qualifications confirmed, Carol set to work at Ngoma running a bush clinic for the local African staff. She was thrown in at the deep end with no-one to turn to for advice, the nearest hospital was over 200 kilometres away, and

12

many of the problems she faced on her first few days, such as malaria, bilharzia and venereal disease were not exactly part of normal nursing training at a British hospital. It took her a few weeks to find her feet and stock the clinic with the correct medicines and basic equipment, but soon she was coping with every type of complaint and injury, delivering babies (she was not trained as a midwife), stitching up drunks and extracting teeth, along with the normal clinic routine. Carol is also a qualified typist, so between the clinic work and running the house, she also undertook much of the station's typing. Whenever she could, she came with me on field trips; even the addition of our son Jonathon to the family in November 1966 did not stop her from being so active.

Early in 1966 I was asked to conduct some field trials with what was then a new immobilising drug called M.99, or Etorphine. We selected the waterbuck as our study animal. They were conveniently close to Ngoma, reasonably abundant and approachable, and when immobilised and marked with collars would form an ideal subject for a behaviour study. After trying a variety of weapons and projectile syringes for delivering the drug, I decided that a crossbow was the most satisfactory and after some initial problems I hit on a perfect 'cocktail' for immobilising waterbuck made of M.99 and the tranquilliser acetylpromazine. I used a similar combination with great success on puku and buffalo, and in 1967 Bill Bainbridge asked me to use my new techniques in the Zambezi Valley to capture young elephants for export to zoos. It was a very successful exercise which I describe in full in Chapter 3.

The Zambezi capture operation was my first real contact with elephants since my visit to Luangwa and it made me even more determined to move on to a full-time elephant study. I returned to Ngoma, completed my basic vegetation map and continued with the waterbuck study, all the time hoping that I would get an opportunity to move into the fascinating arena of the elephant problem. My chance came in 1968. Bill Bainbridge was expanding the whole of the Luangwa Valley research programme and he wanted a zoologist to examine all the relevant material from the hundreds of elephants that were being shot each year. I jumped at it and in March 1968 we left Ngoma for long leave in England before starting work on the project.

My research on the elephant problem, and our life in the Luangwa Valley, forms the basis of this book, but before I go any further, I must digress for a moment to clarify how the elephant problem came into being.

It is a problem common to nearly all the countries in Africa that still have large resident elephant populations; what is more I have every reason to believe that the problem will be intensified in the years to come. To understand how this complex situation arose, one must go back about 400 years and look at Africa before the European settlers arrived. At that time, the greatest variety of large mammals to be found anywhere in the world was to be found over much of the African continent. It must have been a magnificent sight; up to 30 species of grazers and browsers in large numbers feeding together, and from the reports of the very earliest European explorers it seems that each species had its own rôle to play in the functioning of the forest or savanna community where very often two or more species worked together to utilise the vegetation.

The scene was a fascinating complex. Inter-relationships evolved over thousands of years had led to an incredible variation in the habits and structure of the individual species of animals that culminated in a situation where nearly all parts of the plant communities were used for food. The giraffe nibbled on leaves far above the heads of the other browsers, the tiny duiker browsed at the bottom, and a range of species filled the intermediate regions. The grazers were separated as well: the zebra with their strong upper and lower teeth ate the coarse grass that was often too tough for other species, while the wildebeest and hartebeest moved in when the zebra had finished. The warthog went one stage lower and dug below the ground for bulbs and tubers. Then there were yet other species that both grazed and browsed, the elephant itself and the impala being two good examples.

However, once the European settled in Africa there was a surge of development which resulted in an unprecedented reduction of the large mammal populations, mainly because these animals were regarded as an obstacle to the development of the land. South Africa had a particularly bad record. Incredibly heavy slaughter, to provide meat and hides, for sport, and to remove competition for domestic livestock, virtually eliminated larger wild animals from all accessible areas by the late 1800s. Before it was too late and all wildlife had disappeared, national parks and game reserves were established and the wholesale destruction of wildlife was halted. Unfortunately, the respite was temporary. A new threat now emerged in the form of the population explosion of the indigenous African people.

With the arrival of the European in Africa there had been a gradual lowering of the death rate, but at the same time the birth-rate of the African people remained unchanged, precipitating a frightening population explosion (Fig. 1). Today, some of the highest population growth rates in the world are to be found in parts of Africa, with doubling times of less than 25 years.

The position has been further aggravated by an equally dramatic increase in livestock. In far too many places in Africa, this rapidly increasing pressure of both human population and livestock upon the land has resulted in a sharp

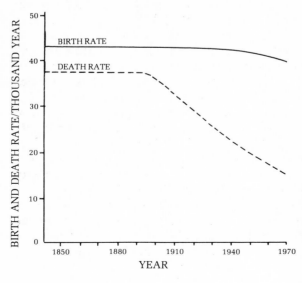

Figure 1. Changes in the birth-rate and death rate of the indigenous African peoples. The birth-rate is the annual number of live births per thousand of the population. The death rate is the annual number of deaths per thousand of the population.

14

decline in soil fertility and a pronounced increase in soil erosion. In addition man is rapidly replacing Africa's natural system, made up of a wonderful variety of plant and animal species, with just a few domestic species of his own choice.

From a system of relative balance, order and abundance, we have moved in many parts of the continent to degradation and chaos, with every indication that several of these changes are irreversible. One of the main reasons for this is man's ignorance of the fragile nature of the land. All forms of primitive cultivation associated with subsistence agriculture extend into marginal areas; in the process plant cover is destroyed and erosion is accelerated to the point where only bare rock remains – hard, sterile and unproductive. On a global basis, this worldwide scourge of man-made deserts now afflicts some 680 million people in 63 countries, and in many parts of Africa the situation has reached crisis proportions. Crude cultivation is not the only culprit. As a desert-maker, man's destruction of trees and woody plants for fuel has few equals – even the elephant problem pales into insignificance against it. For example, in the Sudan 548 million *Acacia* shrubs are used every year just for cooking food, and the majority of these shrubs are pulled up so that regeneration is impossible.

It is perhaps ironic that whereas a great deal of research and ecological expertise has been devoted to the problems associated with the destruction of the woody vegetation by elephants, the devastation caused by man himself, which is far more serious, has been completely ignored until now, when it is almost too late.

Yet another and equally important consequence of the human population explosion has been the increasing isolation of many of the national parks and game reserves, as the growing human population came to occupy the intermediate areas, creating 'island' sanctuaries isolated from one another by a sea of people. It is a process that is still continuing and, if anything, the trend is accelerating.

Attention was first drawn to this 'compression' factor by two scientists working in Uganda, A. C. Brooks and I. O. Buss, in a paper published in 1962. They pointed out that in 1929, 70% of all the land in Uganda was occupied by elephants, but 30 years later this had been reduced to a mere 17%. These drastic changes were attributed to a dramatic increase in the human population.

I believe that this isolation of sanctuaries and compression of range forms the basis of the elephant problem, although in the final chapter of this book I will examine various other current theories. The 'compression' hypothesis implies that as a result of increasing human numbers, the elephants have been forced to move into the sanctuary areas. Animals which used to migrate in and out of sanctuaries according to the seasonal availability of food and water suddenly found they could no longer do so as people had come to settle right across traditional migration routes. Forests were being cleared, and waterholes and riverine areas were being occupied by man and his domestic animals. Even very small human settlements were a positive deterrent. Wildlife populations moving on paths and routes they had used for thousands of years were forced to turn back. Then came animals which used to be resident in the areas outside the sanctuaries, but now had no alternative but to move into the parks and reserves to avoid the molestation they would suffer if they remained outside.

15

Throughout most of Africa the story is the same: a dramatic *redistribution* of the larger mammals, and the elephant more than any other species has been, and still is, at the front of this movement. From the early days when the wildlife sanctuaries carried a variety of browsers and grazers more or less in balance with their habitat, a situation has arisen where several species of large mammals are so numerous that the plant communities are becoming seriously overutilised. To put it simply: the animal populations have exceeded the carrying capacity of the limited areas in which they are forced to live.

Later chapters will deal with all sorts of exciting and fascinating aspects of elephant biology, but in order to complete this introduction to the elephant problem I would like to jump ahead, and select some relevant and important facts and present them here, so that I can give an unbiased view of both sides of the problem.

In several parts of Kenya I could not help but notice that elephants are incredibly careless and extravagant in their feeding habits, well deserving their reputation as the animal bulldozers of the African bush. Subsequently I have seen many other instances of this in Zambia, Rhodesia, Botswana and South Africa. Elephants are very unspecialised feeders, spending at least 12 hours each day grazing and browsing in a wide range of habitats. Bark is stripped from trees for a few mouthfuls of food, and then the tree dies. Large trees are pushed over for the sake of a few leaves or fruit at the top, and then left to rot; sometimes it seems that elephants push over trees just for the fun of it! Their destruction of baobabs in Africa is legendary – perhaps an extreme example of the tremendous devastation they create in the name of daily food consumption. Therefore, it comes as no surprise that when elephants are crowded together, the damage to the plant communities becomes a very serious problem.

In the Chizarira Game Reserve in Rhodesia I have seen vast areas of mufuti (*Brachystegia boehmii*) woodland devastated by elephants. In parts of the Luangwa Valley in Zambia mopane woodland is in a similar state; mature trees are destroyed and the new growth heavily coppiced by constant browsing. In the Tsavo Park in Kenya, an area well-known to wildlife enthusiasts throughout the world, a combination of elephants and fire has resulted in thinning and destruction of large areas of *Commiphora-Acacia* bush, and its replacement by grassland.

This might not appear to matter until you come to appreciate that throughout Africa there is the very real danger that species of trees are close to being *completely* eliminated from wildlife areas as a result of too many elephants. An added complication, as if we did not have enough already, is the annual grass fires which are started both deliberately and accidentally. Such fires prevent the growth of saplings, and so the mature trees that are destroyed are not being replaced.

No natural area anywhere in the world remains unchanged; old trees die, new trees replace them, fires open up woodland and animals are constantly modifying the vegetation. These are the immediate and obvious short-term changes, but there are additional long-term ones. For instance, during the Pleistocene forests expanded and contracted in phase with the climatic cycles. Change is inevitable, indeed it is 'natural'. In short, we must not look upon national parks as areas

16

where we stop or 'freeze' natural changes, because this would be wrong. But if we accept that these sanctuaries are created to conserve a full spectrum of plants and animals that are indigenous to that environment *under conditions as little influenced by man as possible,* then we must also accept that the present rates of change of woodland into open grassland are unnatural changes in that they would *not* have taken place in the absence of man. To return to my theme: our *own* population explosion has created the elephant problem.

What can be done to slow down these habitat changes? By killing large numbers of elephants we should, in theory, considerably reduce the destruction of the vegetation; by eliminating unwanted fires we should help regeneration. It is a two-pronged approach. If, on the other hand, we do nothing, then the chances are that the trees will continue to disappear, and with them will go habitats for a variety of mammals, birds, insects and reptiles.

To be realistic, if a meaningful reduction of elephants is to take place, hundreds will have to be killed inside the boundaries of the very areas that were set aside for their conservation. Have we any alternative? The antagonists of such a proposal believe we have; they advocate a policy of non-intervention by man. They argue that if left to their own devices the elephants and all the other species involved will sort the problem out for themselves. Furthermore, they maintain that the present changes to the vegetation brought about by the elephants are not unnatural and should be regarded as *utilisation* rather than over-utilisation. They point out that tall trees provide browse for only the giraffe and the elephant but a tree coppiced by elephants encourages new growth low down which provides browse for several other species which previously did not have access to it, such as bushbuck and impala.

The antagonists of the elephant culling programme also list the many other positive attributes of the elephants, which, they maintain, are forgotten or overlooked. Elephants push over mature trees, aiding the energy and mineral cycles; their pathways to and from watering points become important bush clearings, often reducing the spread of grass fires; elephants help other animals by opening up new waterholes in dry areas; and they also help plants by playing an important rôle in seed dispersal. There are other examples, too, which I will introduce later. What, say the antagonists, will happen to natural areas if too many elephants are killed, and all these positive attributes removed or reduced?

As convincing as some of these arguments may seem, most biologists now agree that the damage to the vegetation has become excessive, and that positive intervention by man, although an unpalatable prospect, is inevitable.

In spite of all the opposition, the killing of hundreds of elephants has continued, and this has stimulated a new wave of elephant research. After all, where else in the world can a biologist obtain literally hundreds of these large animals for research purposes? My own doctoral thesis was based on a shot sample of over 1 400 elephants, and many of the animals I examined form the basis of the story that follows.

As a result of this intensive effort, we now know far more about the elephant than we did ten years ago, but instead of helping to put an end to the elephant controversy, it has presented new arguments! This came about because of the exciting discovery that the elephant has a kind of built-in birth control

17

mechanism. This fascinating topic forms the basis of a later chapter, but we must consider the bare outlines here, because it adds a new perspective to the elephant problem.

Very briefly, comparative studies in different parts of Africa have revealed that as the elephant population density increases and food becomes scarce, they breed less frequently and produce fewer calves. In uncrowded conditions, with an abundance of food, female elephants reach puberty at about ten years of age, and can continue their reproductive activity until they die of old age at about 60. Within these 50 years they produce one calf every three to four years. But in overcrowded conditions, when food is in short supply, the picture can change dramatically. Puberty may be reached at anywhere between ten and 20 years of age, while females may stop breeding at about 50 before they reach old age. In other words, their effective reproductive life can be reduced by 20 years. But that is not all. Within this period the frequency with which they give birth can also be reduced, from a calf every three to four years, to one every eight to nine.

As might have been anticipated, these observations provided new ammunition for those who had wanted to adopt a laissez-faire policy with the elephant problem. On the strength of these findings they argued more forcefully that if the elephants were left to their own devices, they would indeed sort the problem out for themselves. A whole new dimension has been thrown into the controversy, but is it valid?

Perhaps it would be premature to try to answer that question until we have had a very close look at all the relevant aspects of elephant biology, and tried to dispel some of the myths that surround the animal, myths that have been perpetuated for hundreds of years. For example, a twelfth century Latin bestiary stated: 'There is an animal called an elephant . . . no larger animal can be found. They possess vast intelligence and memory. And they copulate back to back. Elephants remain pregnant for two years, nor do they have babies more than once, nor do they have several at a time, but only one. They live three hundred years . . .' This fascinating little extract is part fact, part fiction, as we shall see.

18

2
Elephant feeding habits and impact on the vegetation

Just how great an impact do elephants really have on the vegetation? This is a vitally important question to answer as it is, after all, the primary reason for concern about the increase in elephant numbers inside the game reserves and national parks.

It is now generally accepted that wherever elephants occur in large numbers, from near desert-like conditions to the high forests of East Africa, they have had a drastic effect on their environment. In places they have been seen to destroy parts of the woody vegetation in a matter of minutes. Although this damage to the trees and forests of Africa has been accentuated in the last decade, and much of it has been concentrated inside wildlife sanctuaries, elephants have always had rather extravagant and wasteful feeding habits.

W. D. Hubbard, one of the first to call attention to this 50 years ago in his observations on the elephants of Northern Rhodesia and Portuguese East Africa, wrote: 'To procure fruit they will travel long distances and when they find a patch of fruit-bearing trees, will lay it waste.'

Observations of this sort have prompted several biologists to suggest that wherever large elephant populations occur there will be a reduction in the diversity of plants in that area. This raises the key question: If woody vegetation is being severely over-utilised and destroyed by elephants inside a game reserve, to what extent is intervention by man necessary and desirable to halt this trend?

By its very nature, a game reserve requires protection by man from man, but the form this protection takes must be determined by the objectives in creating the reserve in the first place – what scientists call the 'aims of management' for the area. Once these have been established and agreed, then it is the duty of the staff concerned to do all they can to try to meet these desired objectives. Let us suppose, for example, that a particular reserve has been set aside so that the full range of plants and animals that are indigenous to that environment are contained in that reserve under conditions as little affected by the presence of man as possible. Let us further assume that one of the components of this system is a large area of woodland. If detailed studies show that this woodland is being destroyed by elephants and that fire is preventing its regeneration, and that both the high elephant population density and the frequent fires are the consequence

19

of 'unnatural' man-made pressures, then it follows that there is a strong case for the reduction of the elephant population and the control of fire. Clearly, one of the first essentials is to get out into the field and *measure* the habitat changes that are occurring so that realistic predictions of the end result of 'leaving it to nature' can be made.

No vegetation communities are static in the sense that they are not changing in their species and age composition. The question to be asked is whether or not a specified rate of change is desirable in terms of the defined management objectives.

Another fundamental component of research is the elephant's feeding habits. A biologist needs to know why elephants select and destroy certain species of trees and leave others untouched: could it be a dietary deficiency or a consequence of disturbance and stress?

These questions were at the back of my mind when Carol, Jonathon and I set out for our first trip to the Luangwa Valley (Map 1) on our return from long leave in England. In actual fact it had not been much of a long leave in the accepted sense. After a short holiday I spent most of my time in Cambridge with Roger Short, reading all I could find on elephants in the libraries and preparing a Ph.D. project outline covering the work I hoped to do on my return to Zambia. As much of it was going to involve the careful processing of post-mortem material, I required good laboratory facilities, so for the next three years I joined the staff of the Agricultural Research Council of Zambia based in Chilanga. (In 1969 the ARC became part of the National Council for Scientific Research in Zambia, and the old name fell away.)

It was over 700 kilometres from our base in Chilanga to my field post near Mfuwe in the Luangwa Valley. Most of this was a rough dirt road from Lusaka to Chipata, and on down into the valley itself, a hot, low-lying area of some 40 000 square kilometres covering parts of the Northern, Eastern and Central Provinces of Zambia. At its widest point the valley is about 96 kilometres across, and it extends over 600 kilometres from Fort Hill near the Malawi border to Feira on the Zambezi River. The middle of the valley is about 580 metres above sea level, and the Luangwa River which changes course nearly every year, is characterised by a beautiful series of ox-bows and lagoons set in a broad alluvial flood plain. To the west of the river the valley is bounded by the sharp, fairly precipitous Muchinga Escarpment which rises to about 1 400 metres above sea level. In contrast the boundary to the east consists of rolling hills, rarely more than 1 000 metres high.

In my first year of work on the elephant project there was no housing available anywhere in the Luangwa, and for our first trip we set off in our Land Rover with caravan in tow. We left early in the morning, optimistically thinking we could get all the way to Chipata with daylight to spare. The road from Lusaka became progressively worse the farther we went, and the caravan bumped and swung wildly behind us. Over the really bad parts of the road we were forced to drive at snail's pace. It was hot and extremely dusty. There had been no rain for at least four months, and when we stopped under the shade of a tree for a midday break, we were horrified to find that all the retaining catches on the caravan windows had sheared through as a result of the continuous vibrations on the dirt road. The windows had been flapping up and down and the combined effect converted the

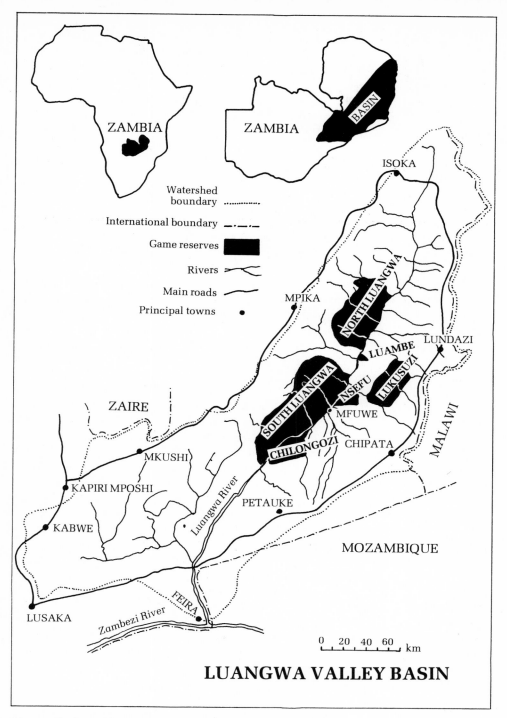

ZAMBIA

ZAMBIA

BASIN

ISOKA

Watershed
boundary ··········

International boundary —·—·—

Game reserves ▬

Rivers

Main roads

Principal towns •

NORTH LUANGWA

LUNDAZI

MPIKA

LUAMBE

LUKUSUZI

ZAIRE

SOUTH LUANGWA

NSEFU

MALAWI

MFUWE

MKUSHI

CHILONGOZI

CHIPATA

KAPIRI MPOSHI

Luangwa River

PETAUKE

KABWE

MOZAMBIQUE

LUSAKA

FEIRA

Zambezi River

0 20 40 60 km

LUANGWA VALLEY BASIN

Map 1. The location of the South Luangwa Game Reserve.

caravan into something like a giant vacuum cleaner designed to take in as much dust as possible!

The interior of our future abode was almost unrecognisable – everything was centimetres deep in thick grey dust. It was impossible to repair the catches with the tools we had, and we continued our journey resigned to the fact that a massive clean-up operation awaited us on arrival.

It was long after dark by the time we got to Chipata where we had made arrangements to spend the night with Pat Martin who had recently arrived as Project Manager for the United Nations Luangwa Valley Survey. After calling in at the local Police Station for directions, we set off for what we hoped would be the final ten minutes of our journey. Carefully following the directions, we turned from the main road onto a narrow track that wound off into the miombo woodland up the side of a hill. The road became progressively steeper, bumpier and narrower, twisting this way and that around rocks and trees. After three or four kilometres it became obvious that this must be the wrong road. We had no idea where the track went to, and if we went on much further there was a real danger of getting completely stuck. We had no alternative but to go back. It was impossible to reverse down the track with the caravan, and with trees and rocks crowding in on one side and with a steep drop on the other, we could not pull off to one side and turn round. In the pitch darkness, Carol and I unhooked the caravan – after we had carefully placed some large stones to stop it shooting off down the hill – and then with a careful combination of pulling, pushing, and moving stones into strategic positions, we managed to manoeuvre the caravan to face downhill.

The Land Rover's turn was next; it could just squeeze past the gap between the caravan and the drop on the side of the hill, and so I backed down the road until I could safely turn round. We hooked up again, and drove back to the Police Station for a second attempt. Jonathon, aged two, had lost interest in all our activities by then and was fast asleep on the front seat. Our life at Kafue had conditioned him to long journeys in hot, bumpy Land Rovers, and it was all just another day to him. We found Pat Martin's house at our second attempt, and it was three hot, dusty, thirsty and tired travellers who woke him up late that night. The next morning we completed the relatively short and straightforward journey to our base in the Luangwa Valley.

First-time visitors to the area are always struck by the pristine beauty of the place. I believe that the Luangwa basin contains some of the finest wildlife country left in the whole African continent. The vegetation, very different to that found in the well-known reserves of East Africa, adds to its attraction. It is relevant to my story, and of interest, to describe the plant communities in a little more detail. On the rocky escarpment and shallow stony soils of the rolling hills are extensive areas of miombo woodland, *Brachystegia*, *Julbernardia* and *Isoberlinia*, a woodland that so often has a low carrying capacity. You can drive for hours through miombo country and see very few large mammals.

The valley has two large grassy plains, the Chifungwe and Lunda, where the red mudstone is mantled with black or dark brown calcareous clay. These plains carry *Setaria eylesii* grassland with scattered *Colophospermum mopane*, a tree known throughout Central Africa simply as 'Mopane' (Plate 1). On the recent

22

Plates 1 and 2. Before the elephant population increased, the Luangwa Valley was noted for its extensive areas of beautiful mopane woodland (Plate 1), but the severe overutilisation of the woodland communities (Plate 2) was one of the main reasons for the establishment of the elephant culling programme.

alluvium, soils vary from seasonally waterlogged clays supporting *Oryza* and *Echinochloa* watergrass formations to deep sandy soils carrying *Acacia-Combretum-Terminalia* woodland savanna or riparian forest. Extensive areas of mopane woodland with a short grass cover are found all over the alluvium, and where there are patches of dark brown sandy soil, *Combretum* thicket or woodland occurs with a good grass cover of *Hyparrhenia* and *Andropogon* species.

The alluvium and ox-bow system have a very high carrying capacity. Each year the Luangwa River comes down in flood replenishing mineral nutrients and maintaining a vigorous plant growth at all stages of succession. The real attraction of Luangwa lies in this area, in and around the spectacular riverside communities. The richly varied scenery is complemented by magnificent herds of elephant, buffalo, hippo, zebra, waterbuck, impala and puku. Black rhino, bushbuck and kudu are also comparatively abundant, making this a veritable wildlife paradise.

A study of elephant feeding habits and their impact on the vegetation was outside my terms of reference, and I did no original work on this aspect at all. Nevertheless, as this is such an important subject, I must discuss it in some detail at this stage of the book, because so much of what follows relates to it. As it happens the elephant problem in Luangwa Valley provides an excellent example of the way in which biologists have come to appreciate the relationship between elephant feeding habits and their destruction of the vegetation. Many of the arguments that follow, although differing in detail, have been raised in similar situations elsewhere in Africa, and have stimulated fundamental and fascinating questions as to the rôle elephants play in an African ecosystem.

As far back as 1934, Captain Charles Pitman carried out the first survey of Northern Rhodesia. He reported even at that stage that in the Luangwa Valley the elephant herds were 'assuming disquietingly large proportions'. Local Africans believed that the numbers had been bolstered at the end of the 1914-1918 War by arrivals from Tanganyika, where troops were causing great disturbance. Pitman observed that the elephants were addicted to bark-chewing and he saw large trees almost completely denuded of bark as a result of their attentions. Before Pitman's survey, at various times between 1912 and 1934, the Luangwa Valley had been closed to the general public and game licences were endorsed to the effect that no hunting was permitted there because of the prevalence of sleeping sickness. The tsetse fly, *Glossina morsitans*, occurred throughout most of the valley, and carried a particularly virulent form of human trypanosomiasis. The movement of elephants into the area and the restriction on the amount of hunting allowed, must have been two of the main factors in the increase in the number of animals, but the actual extent of this must remain open to speculation.

In 1960, Frank Fraser Darling made some very valuable observations on the ecology of the Luangwa that are highly relevant to the arguments that follow. He had surveyed parts of the valley and noted that the riverine and alluvial strip of the Mwaleshi (a small river in the northern area) was the only part of the Luangwa he saw that he felt was overgrazed and overbrowsed. Mopane and other trees had suffered. However, he also pointed out that although mopane trees were browsed back to two metres in height by elephants, this made excellent browse conditions available for other animals. He went on to say ' . . . in my

24

Plate 3. Surrounded by stumps of dead and dying trees, an elephant pushes over yet another mature mopane tree for a mouthful of leaves.

Plate 4. A stately and magnificent baobab tree reduced to a mass of pulp – the result of a combined onslaught by a small herd of elephants in search of food.

view, the elephant is of integral importance in maintaining habitats in usable condition for other animals'. He listed the elephants' functions as path-making, tree-felling, pan-making, soil aeration and seed dispersal. He then made the observation that just as the Luangwa River destroyed trees in its annual changes of course, so did the elephant, but that the word 'destruction' was incorrectly applied to the activity seen in terms of the total environment. In that large setting, the activities of the river and the elephant should be considered constructive because the habitats were kept in a state of diversification.

In 1964, the Department of Game and Fisheries in their Annual Report drew attention to the extent of the damage to the vegetation. It noted that degradation by overgrazing of certain game animals together with the de-stabilisation of the Luangwa by uncontrolled cultivation in the headwaters gave cause for grave concern. Elephants were blamed for most of the changes that were taking place, and it was reported that vast areas of mopane woodland were being converted into open grassland subject to annual devastating grass fires (Plates 2 and 3). Attention was also drawn to the destruction of baobab trees (Plate 4).

In the following year, the Departmental Annual Report stated: 'Under the particular climatic conditions pertaining to the valley the decline of tree cover has not so far resulted in luxurious stands of grass; instead, under the severe feeding pressure, the grasses have been rapidly grazed down to ground level and areas of soil, many square miles in extent, bared to sheet erosion.'

As a result of these reports positive action was taken for the first time to reduce the decline of the woody vegetation and to organise a more detailed research programme. Recommendations were made by experts from the Food and Agricultural Organisation of the United Nations, and an appeal to FAO for a team of experts to begin work on a land use and ecological survey of the entire Luangwa basin was drafted and approved by the Government of Zambia.

It was decided that the survey should be carried out in two stages: an initial reconnaissance by a team of two ecologists who would assess the problem and draw up the plan for the second stage involving an over-all survey of all ecological and conservation aspects of the Luangwa River drainage system. Before the survey started, local Departmental staff continued their field work, and in 1965, on the basis of further observations, Bill Bainbridge and Johnny Uys recommended the initiation of the elephant culling programme which I had witnessed just after my arrival in Zambia in 1965.

In 1966, the FAO team of two experts, D. G. Dodds and D. R. Patton, began work on their survey, and they submitted their report in March 1967. It included recommendations on water resources, game research, fire, tourism, agriculture and education. They also expressed concern about the state of the habitat and the animal populations. Furthermore, they considered it possible that a die-off of animals might occur imminently, and that only an immediate capital reduction of elephant, buffalo and hippo could prevent a possible disaster and death through starvation of hundreds of animals. At the time this was considered quite a drastic recommendation. The formulation of the Plan of Operation for the main Luangwa Valley Conservation and Development Project subsequently followed, and was signed by the Government of Zambia in 1969.

What I have always found really surprising is that up to this point in time, no *quantitative* measurements had been made of the extent of the damage to the woody vegetation or the amount of overgrazing. In fact, several people were beginning to question that a problem existed at all. In 1966, R. M. Lawton, in a roneoed report with a limited circulation within Zambia, pointed out that although a comparison of the aerial photographs of 1951/52 and 1965 did show that some of the scattered trees and shrubs growing in areas of grassland had been destroyed in the past 15 years, the trees in the surrounding areas had remained unchanged. He was very critical of the previous rather subjective studies, and he wrote: 'No ecological evidence has been collected over a period to support the view that the habitat is being destroyed by overgrazing and overbrowsing; it is therefore only based on surmise.' Lawton also noted that although the mopane clays support a few perennial grasses, annuals are more common, and consequently the soil surface under the mopane woodland is bare during the dry season. He emphasised that these bare areas should not be confused with overgrazing.

In the middle of 1968, just before I started my own elephant research in the area, Bill Verboom, an ecologist with many years' experience in tropical regions, visited the Luangwa and wrote some comments on the areas he had examined. His remarks tended to confirm Lawton's observations. For example, Verboom agreed that there was very localised overutilisation of the habitat, but questioned whether this had yet reached serious proportions. He believed that in the tall 'cathedral' mopane, the pushing over of mature trees by elephants was *not* undesirable. In fact, it was utilisation of an available food source, as no other animals could use these tall trees apart from the mopane squirrel.

Referring to the Luangwa bank erosion, he considered this as a natural geological process of a 're-grading' river system, where the banks are cut on the outer curve and deposition occurs on the inner curve. Verboom agreed that there was a lack of regeneration of certain woody species in the riverine areas, but he attributed this to the present high density of various antelope species, and not to fire. He put forward the interesting suggestion that in the past, when the valley had been settled by man with his shifting cultivation, the young very palatable seedlings had a chance to develop and grow as a result of temporary protection. When human settlement was moved out, the antelope moved in, and many of the seedlings lost their chance to develop any further.

Lawton returned to the argument again in 1970, blaming fire as the main source of destruction of the habitat. He described how elephants strip the bark off trees and may ring-bark them as well, killing the stems. He believed that most of these trees would eventually coppice from the roots, and concluded: 'The observations presented in this paper suggest that the habitat is not being destroyed by overgrazing or overbrowsing, but that fire is the main cause of destruction.'

Arguments and counter-arguments such as those that arose in the Luangwa are all too familiar throughout Africa where the elephant problem exists, with each side accusing the other of subjective assessments, while being just as guilty of the same thing. Unfortunately this has led to much of the unnecessary confusion that surrounds elephant culling programmes, and it is only very recently that attempts have been made to rectify this unsatisfactory situation. For example, the final report by the FAO team in the Luangwa Valley *quantified* the rate of damage to trees. Much of the controversy in the Luangwa centred around the damage to the mopane woodland and the FAO team was able to report that the species was being felled at a mean rate of 138 trees/km²/year, or 4% of the standing crop of trees each year. This quantified approach represented a considerable advance over the earlier assessments.

Elsewhere in Africa, this vitally important subject of the impact of elephants on their habitat has received a great deal of attention, and perhaps one of the most outstanding recent studies has been that of Doug Anderson and Brian Walker at the Hostes Nicolle Institute of Wildlife Research in Rhodesia. In addition to measuring the rate of destruction and the amount of utilisation of the vegetation, they attempted to find out why elephants selected certain areas and species for feeding and ignored others. From their studies, it appeared that elephant damage was not related to the chemical constituents analysed in the vegetation and soil, with the exception of a low positive correlation with sodium in the soil.

Anderson and Walker reported that elephants prefer to browse on new regrowth from previously damaged mopane trees, and that they are attracted to areas of favoured riverine vegetation, simultaneously damaging the adjacent mopane woodland. Damage also occurred along drainage lines and routes taken to and from water points. One of their most important conclusions was that in their study area an average of 63% of the total tree population in the three main vegetation types had been either killed or converted to shrubs over the past seven years.

An even more recent study along similar lines was that of Peter Thomson in the Chizarira Game Reserve in Rhodesia, an area to the north of the Hostes Nicolle Institute. In Chizarira, there is a very real danger of the reserve losing its *Brachystegia boehmii* woodland as a result of seasonal overutilisation by elephants. This excessive utilisation did not take place before the mid-sixties, but since then it has been most dramatic, with possibly one of the highest rates of destruction yet recorded.

Thomson surveyed the damage by labelling trees with metal tags so that he could follow their fate. In one area, at the end of 1973, of the original 500 trees sampled, 66,8% were dead, 20,4% were damaged and only 12,8% remained alive and undamaged. However, what made the Chizarira situation different from other elephant problem areas was the fact that nearly all the trees damaged by elephants became vulnerable to attack by insect borers, (even if only a small part of the bark had been removed the wood was broken down rapidly by a succession of these insects). Attack by fungi followed and the trees became susceptible to further damage by wind and fire. Few trees survived these onslaughts and death was almost inevitable.

One of the most striking features of the Chizarira woodland was that much of it consisted of well-grown mature trees of over six metres in height, with an understorey of fire-inhibited regrowth less than 0,5 metres tall. Excavations of the roots of these regrowths revealed thick rootstocks, up to ten centimetres in diameter, and these provided the clue to the structure of the woodland. The rootstocks were covered with scars of former aerial parts that had been burnt back, thereby confirming the rôle of fire in preventing regeneration.

The Chizarira elephant problem is a classic example of the compression hypothesis I mentioned in Chapter One. Thomson described how the Tonga people displaced from the Zambezi Valley by the inundation of the area by Lake Kariba, were resettled in areas south and south east of Chizarira. As a direct result, the elephant population was compressed into the remaining uninhabited areas and game reserve. The fact that people had made their new homes at permanent natural water supplies probably resulted in competition between elephants and man for water during the dry season, further limiting elephants into areas where undisturbed supplies were still available.

Unfortunately, the same Tonga were responsible for most of the fire damage in Chizarira. These people started fires to clear land for cultivation and to stimulate fresh grass growth for domestic stock, but the flames had been carried into the reserve by the prevailing easterly winds. For four consecutive years from 1968, nearly the whole of the reserve was burnt out.

On the basis of Thomson's work, nobody could deny that the destruction of the woodland and the lack of regeneration in Chizarira had reached serious proportions. The undisputed measurements were there for all to see. To slow down this trend, an elephant culling programme and fire control measures were introduced with visible results that fire protection does achieve objectives; there has been a vast regeneration of woodland, and in places the saplings are from one to three metres tall, forming extremely dense stands.

Not all studies of the impact of elephants on the vegetation have recommended intervention by man. In 1974, Harvey Croze, in a survey of the whole Seronera woodland community in Tanzania, determined that elephants were destroying large trees at the rate of 2,5% per year. However, in this case Croze suggested that the regeneration potential was adequate to compensate for loss due to elephant activity and he concluded that the large trees would not disappear.

So far we have considered the impact of the elephants on their habitat without looking at how much they eat, when they eat, and what they eat. One of the first attempts that I have come across at measuring elephant food consumption was that of P.P.M. Offermann in 1953, who published some observations on domesticated African elephants in the Belgian Congo. An adult shackled male elephant had to be given 350 to 400 kilograms of grass and foliage each day, but a great portion of this was scattered or fouled. He estimated that a 20-year-old male did not consume more than 150 kilograms in 24 hours.

From the early sixties up to the present, elephant feeding habits have received attention in many parts of the continent, and the vast literature on the subject is beyond the scope of this book. Our knowledge has advanced considerably since the days of Offermann; in addition to a substantial list of plants that elephants will eat, we now know a great deal more about the quantity and quality of an elephant's diet and how this varies with locality and season. Much of this new information has come from an examination of stomach contents when elephants are killed on culling operations, or from an examination of their droppings. As an example of the former, Dick Laws, a foremost researcher in this field, considers that the optimal daily food requirements of an elephant to be about 6% of the live mass on a wet mass basis. He reached this conclusion after weighing 700 stomachs from elephants shot on culling programmes in Kenya, and went on to

Plate 5. Elephants are noteworthy for their diverse feeding habits. In the wetter summer months they graze on fresh green grass, but in the dry season most of their food is browse, often taken from high up in the taller trees.

Plate 6. In their quest for food, elephants have torn strips of bark from this *Acacia tortilis*. No more than a mouthful of bark was taken, yet the damage was enough to kill the tree.

estimate that an average bull elephant of 5 000 kilograms would require 300 kilograms of food in 24 hours, a cow elephant requiring a correspondingly smaller amount.

Studies such as these have demonstrated the very pronounced seasonal variation in the elephant's diet; after the onset of the rains the grass intake increases significantly falling down to low levels as the dry season progresses.

Yet another approach to the study of elephant feeding habits has been tried by Peter Guy. Working in the Sengwa area of Rhodesia he obtained information on the quantity and quality of food consumed by following elephants on foot during daylight hours for between six and eight hours, observing them through binoculars and keeping a distance of about 40 metres (Plates 5 and 6).

He recorded not only the species of woody plants on which the elephants fed, but also the number of mouthfuls of each species taken, the number of plants of each species from which an elephant fed, the way in which the food was taken from the plants and the parts of the plant that were utilised. With the help of a game scout who had followed the elephants with him, the diets of some of the

Plate 7. The magnificent 'Ahmed'. Today, as a result of ivory exploitation, it is very rare to see elephants carrying tusks of such size and weight.

32

elephants were 'duplicated'. To do this, the plants were collected in a similar way to the actual method of feeding, resulting in a pile of vegetation which approximated the volume from each species the elephant had actually fed upon. These gatherings were subsequently weighed to estimate the total amount of food consumed in a day.

Guy concluded that males ate more than females in both the wet and dry seasons, an adult male elephant eating a mean of about 170 kilograms of food each day, and an adult female about 150 kilograms – less than the estimates made from previous studies. He also concluded that throughout the year there was a 'mean feeding time' per 24 hours of ten hours 30 minutes – again less than earlier estimates. However, these estimates were based on the six to eight hour study periods, with the supposition that the daylight activities continued during the night in the same proportion as they do during the day.

After Guy had completed his studies, J. R. Wyatt and S. K. Eltringham published the results of their 24-hour activity studies of elephants in Rwenzori National Park in Uganda.

In all the 18 elephants they observed, the total amount of time spent in feeding amounted to 74,2%, close to 18 hours in a 24-hour period. They reported that feeding took place at all hours, but that there was usually a pronounced reduction in feeding activity in the early hours between 0400 and 0700. If the elephants in Rhodesia had a similar nocturnal activity pattern to those in Uganda, then Guy's estimate for the quantity of food consumed was rather low.

In Peter Guy's Rhodesian study at Sengwa, he estimated that 56 000 trees were pushed over each year in 390 square kilometres. (Although such a figure sounds quite horrifying, in actual fact it is less than 1% of the total number of trees in the area). He found that males pushed over significantly more trees than females, and ate less from them once the tree had been pushed over. He also found that in both sexes there was a very pronounced preference for feeding below two metres, about 80% of the browsing taking place below this height. His final conclusions and recommendations were that if a culling programme for the area was to be considered, about 40 adult males and 40 members of complete family units should be removed from the estimated population of 270 elephants to halt the deterioration of the woodland.

Another way of finding out what elephants eat is by examining their dung. Malcolm Coe, an Oxford ecologist, working in the Tsavo National Park in Kenya, has made one of the more detailed studies of elephant dung and has gone much further than a basic examination and identification of the plant material present. He recognised the vital importance of dung in many parts of Africa where there are high numbers of large mammals, which contributes a considerable amount of material to the decomposer pathway. Coe measured the defecation rates in various elephants as a basis for estimating the amount of plant material the elephant consumes. He found, for example, that a ten-year-old female produced an average of 5,98 kilograms of dung at each defecation, which gave on average a total of 100,36 kilograms in a 24-hour period. The rate of defecation did not differ significantly between night and day or between animals of different ages. From calculations of this nature it is possible to estimate how much of the available plant material is being used by elephants. Coe calculated that in Tsavo the

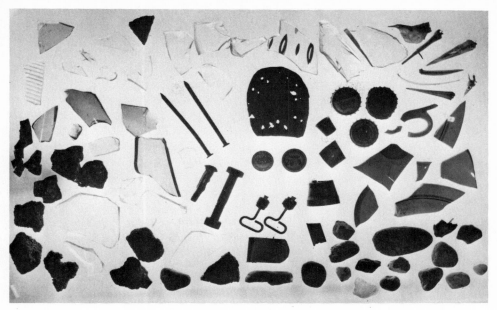

Plate 8. These items were removed from the intestine of an elephant shot in Uganda.

elephants were consuming 22%; a very interesting approach to the study of the quantity of food an elephant will eat.

Visitors to almost any reserve with a big elephant population cannot help but notice that these areas have just one, or a very few species of trees that are highly sought after by elephants. In Chizarira it is *Brachystegia boehmii,* in the Luangwa Valley it is mopane, and nearly everywhere the baobab comes high on the list. Keith McCullagh, who examined the blood from some of the elephants from East Africa, suggested that they might be deficient in essential fatty acids. He found that *Terminalia* and baobab trees in Uganda were both selected by elephants, and these two trees had woody pulp and bark that contained much higher concentrations of linoleic acid than other non-selected trees. In other words, excessive tree damage by elephants could be a natural response to an inadequate fatty-acid intake – an idea that requires further investigation.

I mentioned earlier that several studies have been made of the contents of elephant stomachs, and at times these examinations have produced some unexpected results. As long ago as 1908, T. Codrington exhibited a collection of stones taken from the stomach of an elephant shot in Northern Rhodesia. He counted a total of 168 stones, with a mass of 3,6 kilograms. I recorded a similar case in a young bull elephant shot in Chizarira in Rhodesia; its stomach contained 161 stones with a mass of 1,64 kilograms.

Overleaf: **Plate 9.** It is often difficult to determine the sex of an elephant in the field. The male has no scrotum, and the testes are permanently located inside the body cavity. One of the most useful guides is the shape of the forehead; this is well illustrated in these two young males, where it curves smoothly forward and downwards in contrast to the 'peaked' forehead of the females.

When elephants pull out tufts of grass, it is quite common to see them shaking the tufts to dislodge earth and stones attached to the roots, and it seems likely that sometimes a few stones are accidentally swallowed.

One of the most unusual records I have come across of stomach contents was given to me by Roger Short. In 1965, a young male elephant lived on the Mweya Peninsula in Uganda, and for some time was known to raid the dustbins of the houses at night. Eventually the animal had to be shot, and an examination of its stomach revealed, among other items, broken glass, beer bottle tops, nuts, bolts, fish bones, a 50c piece, one ½ ounce weight, a sardine tin opener, the heel of a shoe, two six inch nails, a collection of stones, the base of a light bulb, and tin foil from wine bottles! (Plate 8.)

Before leaving the subject of elephant feeding habits and the effect on vegetation, it is vital to stress the dangers inherent in a narrow approach to the problem; to put it another way, the absolute necessity for broad-based research – a point that was brought home by David Western's work in Amboseli.

In the early 1960's the extensive fever tree woodland (*Acacia xanthophloea*) in parts of Amboseli started to deteriorate. The most obvious cause seemed to be overgrazing by livestock, but a number of wildlife authorities were claiming that the decline of woodland was caused by elephant damage. Western was not prepared simply to accept that another 'elephant problem' existed, so he began examining soil samples throughout the area. In every case, the dead or dying stands of trees were associated with high salinity levels, while those in good condition were associated with low salinity. As the salinity around a plant increases, it becomes more difficult for its roots to draw up water, and there comes a time when the plant dies. In Amboseli the salinity had increased because the water table had *risen* in the last decade, introducing high salt levels into the tree roots which eventually caused their death.

Exposed fossil beds containing abundant fish fossils in the area provided good evidence that a large part of Amboseli was extensively flooded in the recent past. Furthermore, the alteration of fish fossil horizons with mammalian fossils, such as antelope, indicated that Amboseli has undergone long-term flooding/dessication cycles, and these must have occurred a number of times. The higher water table had caused the death of the trees, and for once the elephant was not to blame.

3
Elephant culling

For the next two years, our life in the dry season centred around the elephant culling programme, and we positioned our caravan under a huge spreading fig tree on the banks of the Luangwa River, a short distance away from the abattoir where the dead elephants were processed.

It was a strange contrast: upstream from our camp was primeval bush, Luangwa as it should be – and downstream and immediately next to us was the abattoir, with throbbing generators providing electricity for night-time work and power for a massive refrigeration plant that was busy turning elephants into unrecognisable slabs of deep-frozen red meat.

In the hour before sunset I would often take Carol and Jonathon for a walk upstream away from the abattoir. We would jump from sand bank to sand bank along the meandering river course itself. The river never stopped flowing, but in the dry season it always dropped way down compared with its torrent at the height of the rains. Throughout the year several stretches of deep water remained, and these contained grunting herds of hippo and many crocodiles as well. Luangwa was renowned for both. In our walks we would nearly always see elephant, impala, waterbuck and buffalo coming down to drink at the river, invariably accompanied by the honking of a flight of Egyptian geese. A spectacular colony of over 300 carmine bee-eaters nested close by in the exposed banks of the river at the end of each dry season, and their harsh twittering could be heard from a long way off, their superb plumage a celebration of pinks and reds. But the highlight of our walks was the sunset at the end – a time when the whole valley was at peace with the world, a time when the shooting, killing, rushing, cutting and processing associated with the elephant culling programme seemed to be far removed from the realities of our day-to-day life.

As the culling of elephants got underway, most conservationists in Zambia accepted the need for it, but there was still a vociferous minority who opposed the whole concept. This was not surprising; the slaughter of literally hundreds of

Overleaf: **Plate 10.** Solitary elephants are almost invariably males who have left the family unit at puberty. The bachelor groups they form are very temporary aggregations.

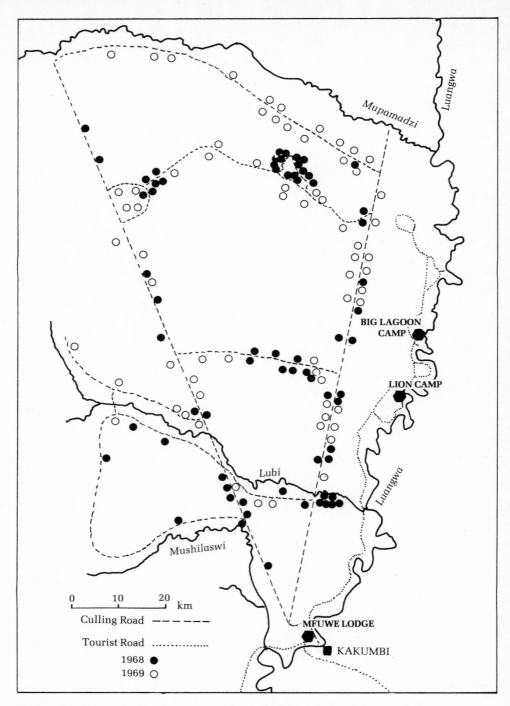

Map 2. The abattoir at Kakumbi was situated outside the South Game Reserve. Elephants were shot on the culling roads away from the tourist roads. Each dot indicates where elephants were shot in 1968 and 1969.

42

elephants in a short space of time is extremely distasteful, even more so perhaps when the killing takes place inside the boundaries of game reserves.

When such magnificent creatures are being killed in their hundreds, it is only too easy to use emotion as a platform to advocate a halt, and this can gain wide support. There can be no doubt that much of the emotion is based on exaggeration and ill-informed accounts of how and why the elephants are killed, and I am convinced that it is in the interest of wildlife conservation to put the record straight by describing a typical culling operation in objective, unemotional terms.

It is strange that biologists seem reluctant to use the verb 'to kill'. Rather than say 'One hundred elephants were killed for habitat protection purposes', they go to extraordinary lengths to avoid the use of that simple and unambiguous verb. The literature is full of ponderous euphemisms such as 'elephant population reduction operations' and 'elephant capital removal programmes'. Even such simple words as 'culling' and 'cropping' have come to be regarded as interchangeable in the elephant world, which is far from the truth. Cropping has a definite 'sustained yield' element which is certainly not what most wildlife ecologists have in mind.

On the whole, elephant culling programmes throughout the continent have followed similar phases in the growth and development of techniques. The main differences have been in the methods of disposal of the elephant carcasses.

At Luangwa the well-defined rainy season in the valley was a major influence on the timing of nearly all the activities that took place there. The rains usually came early in November, and soon afterwards many of the rivers and streams became impassable making it all too easy for vehicles to bog down in the wet, sticky, muddy soil so that the only way to move around was on foot. In effect, the rains limited vehicle movement and access to the dry months of the year: from May or June to the end of October, and these were the only months in which culling was feasible. Unfortunately they were also the only months in which the valley was open to tourists, and it was inevitable that a conflict should arise between the two activities.

From 1965 to 1969, the culling programme was restricted to the South Game Reserve in Luangwa, and 1 464 elephants were killed during this period. The South Game Reserve was also the area with the highest density of tourist camps and roads, and at the start of the programme it was decided that rather than close the valley to visitors, the culling operation and tourism would run literally side by side. To meet these requirements, a special network of roads was constructed out of sight and away from all the main tourist roads, and it was on this special network of roads that the elephants were killed (see Map 2).

Overleaf: **Plate 11.** A tusk forms a useful lever to prize bark from a tree; a wrench with the trunk completes the damage.
Plate 12. Tusk eruption is a useful field guide for age determination. When the tusks first become visible, a young elephant is about 30 months old. The subsequent pattern of growth is extremely variable, and it is virtually impossible to age older elephants on the basis of tusk length or shape.
Plate 13. Play is an integral part of the social life of young elephants: rolling and gambolling in the mud and slapping each other with their trunks, it is not unusual for teenage bulls to mount each other, an activity that may take place at any time during a romp.

Plate 14. The Luangwa Valley abattoir, situated on the banks of the Luangwa River opposite the South Game Reserve.
Plate 15. The hunting team, armed with a 'Cap-Chur' gun and rifles for back-up support, prepare to dart an elephant.

In a country such as Zambia, which has in places a chronic shortage of protein, it would be politically and morally unacceptable to kill a large number of elephants and then to leave the meat in the field. Accordingly it was decided that all the carcasses should be processed for human consumption. From consultations with the retail trade on what would be the most readily marketable form for the product, it became evident that frozen fillets of elephant meat would be preferable to canned or the traditional smoke-dried products. What is more, the Veterinary Department in Zambia made it clear that all the elephant meat must pass the standard meat inspection procedure, whether sold in town or given away free. Consequently, a centrally situated abattoir had to be built, incorporat-

46

ing a deep-freeze chamber, to which the elephants killed in the field could be transported for processing.

There were several priorities that dictated the siting of the abattoir. First of all it was vital to get the carcasses out of the sun and back to the abattoir for processing before the meat started to deteriorate, so it had to be as close as possible to the culling area. Another factor was that materials had to be brought in to build the plant, while the meat had to be transported to the main centres after processing. This further restricted potential sites to a position close to the only good road out of the valley from Mfuwe to Chipata. An additional complication was that the plant required a good water supply and had to be in a position where the water effluent from the factory could be drained back into the main river channel. Finally the abattoir had to be on a site well above the flood level of the river. After careful observations in the wet season, an ideal site was found near a big baobab on the banks of the Luangwa near Kakumbi, opposite Mfuwe and outside the South Game Reserve (see Map 2 and Plate 14). The baobab is extremely sensitive to waterlogged conditions, and is unable to stand flooding even for very short periods. We could therefore be reasonably certain that the site on which the abattoir was to be built had not been flooded during the life of the tree, which was probably several centuries.

When culling started in 1965, one of the main concerns of the Game Department staff was to find a method of killing the elephants with as little disturbance as possible. It was obviously undesirable to have wounded or agitated elephants moving the comparatively short distance from the culling area across to the tourist roads, more so since in some places visitors were walking through the bush on conducted tours. For this reason rifles were rejected and from the start of the operation up to the first part of the 1968 dry season, elephants were killed by darting with a 'Cap-Chur' dart containing a massive overdose of a drug known as succinylcholine chloride (Plate 15).

At the time, there were believed to be two main advantages to this technique. Firstly, the elephants could be hit anywhere on their bodies and, providing that a good deep intramuscular injection of the drug occurred, they would become immobilised within three minutes of darting. Any elephant that did not die soon afterwards from paralysis of the respiratory muscles was killed by a brain shot with a 9mm pistol. The 'Cap-Chur' gun that fired the dart made very little noise, and there was no danger of wounded animals escaping. Secondly, the drug succinylcholine chloride is rapidly broken down into harmless by-products, which makes the meat quite safe for human consumption.

During this period, incomplete or very occasionally complete small family units were taken, and bachelor groups were avoided. I will be considering aspects of elephant social life in more detail later, but it is necessary for the purposes of this chapter and those following, to give a very basic outline of elephant society.

Overleaf: **Plate 16.** Elephant social life is essentially matriarchal, and a basic family unit is organised around an adult cow and her own offspring of both sexes. At puberty, males leave the family unit and join or form small bachelor groups. Most of these elephants have actively secreting temporal glands (see p. 145).

A family unit normally consists of an adult female and her offspring or a number of closely related females and their offspring. Males stay with these family units until puberty when they leave and join or form bachelor herds of varying size. The only time an adult sexually mature bull will join a family unit is when one of the females happens to be in oestrus. Thus the family unit is essentially matriarchal, with the oldest cow in the group usually initiating activities of movement, such as flight or fight. This means that when a family unit is disturbed, there is an immediate tendency for all members of the unit to bunch around the lead cow. If she stays, the group will remain close by her side. If she breaks and runs, the remainder of the family unit will follow. In contrast, the members of a bachelor herd tend to react as individuals when shooting starts, running off in all directions with complete disregard for the other members of the group.

Up until 1968, the culling in the Luangwa Valley removed incomplete, or very occasionally complete family units. In the former case, the culling was not selective. It was usually the elephants first and nearest to the hunters that were darted, and sometimes this included the lead cow. This must have been very traumatic for the elephants; they were chased for a short distance and then three or four were darted and killed. If the lead cows are killed from a number of family units, there is evidence to suggest that these leaderless groups join together and mill around as disorientated larger groups for some time afterwards, creating even greater damage to the habitat because of their erratic movement and restless feeding.

Early in 1968, following a reappraisal of the existing culling technique it was realised that darting with succinylcholine chloride was not the best method – and it was certainly not the most humane. Only three or four elephants could be killed at a time, and when the larger family units were hunted, several elephants would escape, causing a great commotion in the process. But the most compelling reason for changing the technique was the need for a 'random sample' of the population for the many biological studies that were under way. Ideally, whole family units, regardless of size, should be eliminated. In other words the hunting party had to try and ensure that they killed all the members of the first family unit they encountered each day. This could not be done by darting, and so for the remainder of 1968 and for the whole of 1969, all elephants were shot with a heavy calibre rifle, and complete family units were eliminated (Fig. 2).

When this change took place in 1968, Bob Langeveld was in charge of the four-man hunting team. He carried a .470 double barrel rifle, and his gun-bearer an identical rifle. A second hunter supported Langeveld, but he usually only fired in emergencies. The fourth man carried a heavy spear to bleed the elephants as soon as possible after death. Each day the team set out by Land Rover on the culling road network, and drove until a family unit was located. They then approached their target on foot.

Langeveld's technique was to try and wait until the lead cow charged and then to shoot her, usually with a brain shot. The fact that the lead cow had charged very often had the effect of making the remaining members of the family unit bunch together, greatly facilitating shooting. Whenever possible, all elephants were brain shot, but if they turned and ran off they were killed by a heart shot.

50

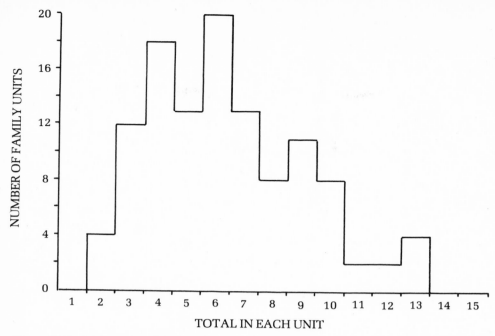

Figure 2. The total number of elephants in each of the family units that were killed in the Luangwa Valley culling programme.

The overall disturbance factor was very small. It was not uncommon for a complete group of ten or more animals to be eliminated, while less than a kilometre away another family unit carried on feeding undisturbed.

In 1968, approximately 1,1 rounds of ammunition were used per elephant, but in 1969 there was an increase to 1,4 rounds. These statistics well illustrate the accuracy of the shooting – indeed, most elephants were killed with a single shot. The very small elephants were downed with a 9mm pistol. The hunters usually shot the first family unit found, but in some cases groups of 20 or more were avoided: to start with, it was extremely difficult to kill a group that size, and the abattoir had problems handling so many carcasses when they arrived en masse. The largest group culled was 26.

Fears have been expressed that from the scientific point of view this selective sampling would influence the final results and conclusions. However, there is now a considerable body of evidence from various sources to show that these larger groups are simply an aggregation of two or more smaller family units. In other words, the method of sampling and culling used in the Luangwa can be taken as a representative cross-section of the female population and pre-pubertal males.

As all the elephants were destined for human consumption, they had to be

Overleaf: **Plate 17.** Elephants usually drink at least once every 24 hours, perhaps even more frequently under very hot and dry conditions. Several family units often come together at a waterhole, and will intermingle quite freely with one another.

Plate 18. An elephant carcass has just been loaded onto a trailer prior to the journey to the abattoir. A tarpaulin keeps off dust and hides the animals from tourists.

bled as soon as possible after death, and this was done by cutting their throats with a spear. If the research team wanted fresh blood samples for any subsequent analysis, this was the time when it was collected. At this stage of the operation, all the elephants were given a serial number, usually marked on their ears with chalk, or on their toe-nails with ink – one of the few places where a number remained visible at the end of the dusty journey back to the abattoir. The object of this exercise was to record the composition and identity of each family unit in the field so that all these animals could be identified on arrival at the abattoir.

The carcasses were then loaded onto tractor-drawn trailers or onto modified Leyland seven-ton flats by means of power-operated winches, and sent as soon as possible to the abattoir (Plate 18). The journey took anything up to five hours, and very often the carcasses would arrive long after dark. The heavily laden vehicles moved down the network of culling roads, around the back of the main tourist lodge at Mfuwe, and onto the banks of the Luangwa River, where one by one they were pulled across the river on a pontoon. At this point a siren at the abattoir announced that the elephants had come, and that work was about to begin.

The sound of that siren is a noise Carol and I will never forget as long as we live.

When the elephants were being processed it was essential that I attend the whole procedure to gather as much information as possible. It took me at least an hour to get organised in the small laboratory next to the abattoir before the first elephant arrived, and long after the final animal had been processed for market I was still working on dissections, labelling of specimens and age determinations from the lower jaws. On several occasions we worked 18 hours without a break,

54

then snatched a few hours of sleep before the siren shattered the peace and quiet of Luangwa and brought us all running back to work.

Outside the entrance of the main hall was a 10-ton gantry fitted with a 7-ton crane weigher graduated in 100 lb units. On arrival each recovery vehicle parked underneath the gantry so that the elephants could be individually removed and weighed, and for the first time in Africa, the total body masses were taken from a large sample of elephants. Following weighing, the carcasses were lowered to the floor, and then pulled into the main hall by means of a power-operated winch. At the same time, all the mud and dust was washed off. The next step was to remove the lower jaws and eyes for age-determination studies, and to take body measurements. The lactational status was noted, and when possible milk samples were collected. The tusks were carefully marked for weighing and measuring later.

The main hall of the abattoir was about 20 metres long by ten metres wide, and from the gantries inside the hall hung a system of blocks and tackle to facilitate the lifting and handling of the carcasses. A highly skilled team of African workers dealt with all stages of the processing during which waste was kept to a minimum, and strict discipline and rules of hygiene were enforced at all times. The elephants were washed, skinned and dismembered, and the meat then left the main chamber on meat rails to enter the pre-chiller where the temperature was 0 °C. After the pre-chiller, the meat was boned, the fillets made up into 23 kilogram packs, and then deep frozen in a large chamber which could hold up to 15 tons of filleted meat at a time. The skin was salted and sold to make high quality leather goods.

With the exception of the collection of blood and milk, body measurements, eyes and lower jaws and tusks, all the material a population biologist wants to collect from an elephant is inside the body cavity – or closely attached to its rear end. To avoid contamination of the meat, the abdominal cavity was never opened in the main hall of the abattoir, but was moved on castor-wheeled trolleys to a degutting shed to one side of the main hall, and it was here and in a small laboratory nearby that I did nearly all my collecting of material. It was at this point of the operation that we opened the abdominal cavity to remove parts of the reproductive tract together with any other body organs we required. A continuous supply of running water through the degutting shed carried away the contents of the intestines together with blood, scraps of meat and other effluent from the main hall of the abattoir to the Luangwa. Where the big effluent pipe ran into the river, crocodiles in their hundreds waited their turn for the stream of scraps. Any unwanted larger parts of the body cavity together with the skull and bones were dumped about nine kilometres away in a clearing in the mopane woodland, again well out of sight of tourists.

Deep-frozen elephant meat was taken to Lusaka by road in a refrigerated truck about once a week, and the meat sold along the line of rail in the main towns.

Much of the credit for the ambitious nature of the Luangwa culling scheme

Overleaf: **Plate 19.** An elephant's trunk is an extremely versatile organ, an amazing combination of mobility, strength and delicate control. It is vital to the animal, being used for drinking, feeding, carrying, smelling, and also as an offensive weapon and vocal organ.

must go to two men: Bill Bainbridge, who initiated many of the ideas associated with the project, and Jack Botha, the abattoir manager. Botha designed and built the abattoir, trained and disciplined the large staff, and gained wide respect for his hard work and ingenious innovations under far from ideal working conditions. He lived at the plant for the duration of its operation, and was always on hand when any problems arose. There were of course many other individuals associated with both the culling programme and the running of the abattoir – hunters, mechanics, meat inspectors and a range of biologists and veterinarians who stayed for varying lengths of time. I must, however, acknowledge in particular the help I received from two German vets at the abattoir – Peter Albl and Jim Dillman. Although all of us were busy with our own studies, we found time to work together on a variety of minor projects and, whenever we could, collected additional specimens or data we thought might be of help to the others. On the whole, there was a very good team spirit; without it work would have been almost impossible as it was only too easy for tempers to become frayed when fatigue set in late at night in the unpleasant atmosphere of the abattoir.

Carol gave me wonderful support especially when we were working under pressure, and she kept up a constant supply of black coffee and sandwiches. In retrospect, this must have contravened every health regulation in the book, considering the working conditions in the de-gutting shed; nevertheless, such sustenance and cheerful encouragement were extremely welcome.

From the research point of view, the only disadvantage of the Luangwa method of processing the carcasses was that three to 20 hours elapsed between bleeding in the field and opening the body cavity in the abattoir. After ten hours or so, the abdominal cavities became very distended with gas. Opening them up was a smelly, unpleasant – and at times hazardous – task. Even more important was the fact that some of the tissues began to decompose under these extreme conditions which rendered them of rather limited value for a more detailed microscopic study of their structure, and as a result much useful information was lost. But, in spite of this disadvantage, a great deal of extremely valuable information was obtained from the culling operation, and there can be no doubt that the whole processing operation greatly facilitated the various biological studies. Measuring, weighing and dissecting just one elephant in the hot sun is very hard work and when 12 or more are killed in one day and left in the field, it becomes impossible for a small research team to collect a full range of material from each animal.

With the exception of the Kruger National Park, other elephant culling programmes in Uganda, Kenya, Tanzania and Rhodesia have gone ahead on a large scale without a fixed abattoir. In these operations, the meat was either sold fresh to the local residents, or dried as biltong and taken away for sale in the towns. In most cases, the skins were also collected and salted, and stacked for future sale. Understandably biological studies become much more difficult under these conditions, and larger research teams are required for a comprehensive collection of material. On the other hand there is no doubt that the absence of an abattoir reduces capital costs substantially, and gives the culling team a much greater degree of flexibility. The capital and recurrent expenditure for the Luangwa abattoir and the fleet of recovery vehicles, and a host of other factors

58

such as the depreciation of the plant and equipment have never been calculated. Furthermore the whole plant stood idle for at least six months of the year during and just after the rainy season. From the point of view of the actual culling programme, the fixed position of the abattoir and the limited network of hunting and recovery roads presented several other drawbacks. In the hot low-lying valley, carcasses had to be returned to the abattoir as soon as possible to prevent them being condemned as unfit for human consumption. This placed very real physical limitations on where elephants could be shot. And as many of the culling roads ran close to tourist roads, certain areas became depleted of elephants and some regular visitors to the area complained.

Yet another disadvantage of a fixed abattoir arises from the possibility that culling in a fixed area could result in a greater part of one or two subpopulations being drastically reduced, while other unit populations remain totally unaffected. This would be bad management in terms of a wildlife reserve, and if the culling area was close to or contained the main tourist roads, then tourism could suffer.

Extrapolations from experience gained in the Luangwa led to an interesting conclusion that if elephants are to be killed, and the meat used by man, the production of dried meat (biltong) by the traditional African methods should be encouraged, studied scientifically, and extended. Such products find a ready market, and their nutritive value is generally as good as many of the products made by advanced techniques. On this basis capital costs are reduced, and the need to build a fixed abattoir, with all its inherent disadvantages, falls away.

At the end of our first year in Luangwa, Carol and I decided that there were too many problems associated with living in Chilanga and travelling down to the valley for each culling session, and so we moved to Chipata, where we got a house in the village next door to Pat Martin, the Luangwa Valley Project Manager. Home was now just an hour's drive away from the valley, and I was able to set up a small laboratory in Chipata and start processing some of my material. It was during this period that Roger Short, who was supervising my Ph.D., flew out from Cambridge and spent two weeks working with me in the field. Luckily the abattoir was in full swing during his visit, and I picked up many new useful techniques and ideas from him. The results of all this work form the basis of the rest of this book, but before we move on, I must go back in time to the elephant capture operation in the Zambezi Valley. I do this because people constantly ask me if live capture and translocation of elephants could not be an alternative to killing so many animals. Unfortunately, the answer is no. The only worthwhile outlet for captured elephants is zoos, and this market is close to saturated. Furthermore, the capture and movement of elephants is an expensive and time-consuming exercise, which cannot begin to compare with a culling programme.

The Zambezi capture operation was intended simply as a feasibility study to try out capture techniques and to investigate the problems of moving and caring for very young elephants. As several people have considered similar capture

Overleaf: **Plate 20.** Two young bulls engage in a mock battle for supremacy. Records of elephants actually fighting with one another are few and far between.

operations as an alternative, or rather a supplement, to elephant culling, let me describe my experiences on the Zambezi operation.

The whole exercise had been organised by Peter Morris, Chief Game Ranger of the Department, and it all took place in a wild and isolated part of the Zambezi Valley within a few kilometres of Musika camp, and about 180 kilometres from Lusaka. During our first trip in September 1966, we carried out a preliminary trial prior to the major exercise in May 1967. Peter Morris had gone on ahead of me to make all the arrangements for the care and movement of the elephants. I followed him two days later. My job was to fly in the helicopter and select and dart suitable young elephants. The whole exercise had to be run to a tight schedule since a helicopter is expensive to hire, and we could not afford to have it sitting on the ground inactive while we got ourselves organised.

I left Lusaka in the very early morning, planning to arrive at Musika and start darting that afternoon. Ninety kilometres from Lusaka on the road to Chipata I turned off the main road onto a very steep and narrow track that wound its way down the escarpment to Musika. About halfway down, as I was approaching a particularly steep hill and sharp corner, my brakes, which had been giving me trouble ever since I had left Lusaka that morning, failed completely. I was luckily able to pull to one side and bring the vehicle to a halt. Effective repairs were impossible where I was, and I was still at least 30 kilometres from our base camp. On top of this I knew that the whole capture operation was due to start in about two hours time, and could not get underway until I arrived. I decided to continue. I put the Land Rover into low ratio and first gear, and with my Game Guard using his foot to jam the low ratio lever in the correct position, made it on time using the engine as a brake. It was not an experience I would like to repeat!

We had already discussed plans for the capture programme, and as I loaded up my first darts with a mixture of M.99 and acetylpromazine, two of our Land Rovers drove off in the direction of an open grassy plain not far from the camp, where Game Guards had seen several elephant family units earlier that morning. I climbed into the helicopter with the pilot, Cliff Sleight, and adjusted my seat belt to allow me to lean well over the side of the helicopter to get a clear shot.

For our first animal we decided to go for a fairly big calf which made a reasonably easy target and would also settle the question of whether there were likely to be any real problems driving off an irate mother from her recumbent juvenile. The first approach was almost too easy. There were six elephants moving slowly across an open area within a kilometre of the Land Rovers, with a calf, its tusks just visible, at the back of the group. As soon as they heard the helicopter, they started running, and as we came down low, they were strung out in single file, with the calf we wanted bringing up the rear. It was a simple matter to fly the helicopter at the same pace as the elephant, positioning it above and to the left of the moving animal. My first shot went straight into the shoulder, and to avoid any further disturbance we pulled away and landed nearby to watch what happened. Within six minutes the darted calf became ataxic, moving around in circles and obviously under the influence of the drug. It collapsed eight minutes later, but by then its mother had returned, and was reluctant to leave. An approach by Land Rover was out of the question, and it took us five minutes of low flying in the helicopter to chase the cow away.

62

The calf was much bigger than I had first thought – 213 centimetres at the shoulder, with tusks 20 centimetres long. I injected the antidote, M.285, into the ear vein, and a few minutes later the animal got to its feet and moved off. On reflection, I am quite surprised that the cow showed such a strong maternal instinct towards such a large calf. Only then, too, did I begin to appreciate the difficulties of judging the size of young elephants from the air. Having learnt from our experience, we decided to restrict ourselves to those elephants which could just walk under their mothers, or, if they were bigger than this, had no tusks visible externally. We had already decided not to try and capture very young elephants because of the problems involved in finding an acceptable alternative to elephant's milk. Our first attempt had been somewhat discouraging in terms of the reaction of the cows to their immobilised offspring, and we anticipated much more trouble with very young calves.

I returned to the helicopter for our first real capture attempt. After a few minutes' flying, we located a family unit of five out in the open. In the middle of the group was one youngster still able to walk under its mother – the ideal size for our purposes. As the helicopter came down low the elephants panicked and ran for the trees. My first shot at the calf passed just over its back, and it was five minutes before I could try again. The family unit was now milling around under some big *Acacia* trees which made it impossible to get the helicopter in close enough for a second shot. Eventually the lead cow made a dash for the open, the others following close behind. We came down low to try again. As we approached the group, one of the cows gave us a nasty shock; she spun round and reached up at us with her trunk, trying to knock or pull us out of the sky. Cliff was quite shaken, and he pulled the helicopter up into a steep climb to get out of her reach. However, by now the whole group was right out in the open. We had clearly created a tremendous disturbance for the elephants were well spread out, and the very young elephant we were after was on its own about 100 metres behind the others, struggling frantically to keep up.

I had an easy shot – there were no trees or other elephants to worry about – and the dart appeared to go straight in behind the animal's shoulder. Within three minutes, the first effects of the drug were apparent, and 11 minutes later it was down. From where we were in the helicopter it appeared to be completely immobilised. We hovered over the spot to guide the Land Rovers in to pick the animal up, and then landed in an opening about 200 metres away. The rest of the family unit had disappeared. We were all feeling very pleased with ourselves at our first success – our target was ten elephants, and at this rate we thought we would complete the whole exercise in two or three days. We did not realise that our troubles were just about to begin!

By the time I reached the immobilised elephant, Peter Morris and his party were already there, backing up one of the vehicles to load the elephant, and organising labourers from the other vehicle to help lift it on board. It was a young female, probably weighing about 350 kilograms, and just what we wanted. Then, without warning, she staggered to her feet, and stood, swaying from side to side. The African labourers scattered in all directions; even Peter Morris looked rather apprehensive – a 350 kilogram elephant is no mean adversary!

Before anyone could decide what to do, the young elephant staggered off in

the direction she had been travelling when darted, a Game Guard holding on to her tail and being pulled along as if he didn't exist. I rushed back to the helicopter for some more M.99 and a syringe, and set off in hot pursuit. (We discovered later that my dart had gone in at a slight angle, giving a subcutaneous rather than a good intramuscular injection.) By the time I had caught up, there were two Game Guards and Peter Morris doing all they could to slow the elephant down. I managed to give a quick intramuscular injection by hand and after five minutes our young elephant was immobilised once again.

We promptly christened her Leslie, and after much panting and heaving loaded her up for the journey back to Musika. By now we were all hot, scratched, and not quite as confident as we had been earlier. We felt we had had enough for one day and followed Leslie in convoy back to our base camp.

The trip passed without incident. Leslie was lying on her side on top of grass-filled sacks as we had decided against using a crate for this first stage of her journey which took us over very rough bumpy terrain where a violently swaying crate on the back of a Land Rover would have been traumatic for the young elephants and could well have resulted in injury.

At Musika, Leslie was unloaded inside the stockade Peter had finished constructing the day before, and I gave her an injection of the antidote, M.285, into the ear vein. She was on her feet almost immediately, and stood quietly in one corner, making no attempt to escape (Plate 22). We stood watching her for a few minutes and, satisfied that all seemed well, went back to the camp to discuss our plans for the next day.

No sooner had we sat down when one of the Game Guards yelled for help — Leslie had escaped. With very little effort she had broken through the stockade, and was running off upstream along the banks of the Zambezi as fast as she could go. It was impossible to chase her on foot. Cliff Sleight and I rushed for the helicopter to give chase. She was easy to find, but very difficult to dart, as she moved through thicket and under the tall *Acacia albida* along the river banks. After nearly 20 minutes' flying I got in a shot, but this time it was nearly ten minutes before she went down, not in an open short grass area as before, but at the bottom of a steep bank in long grass, with almost impenetrable thicket between her and the pursuing Land Rovers. It took us a further two hours to get Leslie back to the stockade. Meanwhile, Peter had organised the labourers to repair the damaged area, and to strengthen any other points of weakness, and we were confident that this time we had her for good. Leslie was as exhausted as we were — she stood quite still showing no interest in food, water or people, and we retired to our camp for a second time.

A few minutes before sunset another shout went up from the stockade. Leslie was making a second attempt at escape. We could hear wood splintering as we rushed over, but by the time we got there she was out, and it was a very determined young elephant that rushed past us in the direction of the river. The re-capture operation got underway again, but without success. Darkness caught

Plate 21. Cleanliness is as important in the elephants as it is in other animals. When an elephant comes to water, it first drinks and then washes, either wallowing in the water, or using its trunk to squirt water all over its body.

65

Plate 22. A young elephant, estimated to be about three months old, captured by darting from a helicopter in the Zambezi Valley.
Plate 23. Within a few days of capture, young elephants have no fear of man.

up with us, and we had no alternative but to let her go. She was last seen walking very purposefully towards the escarpment.

We had learnt our lesson. The next two days were spent rebuilding the stockade with closely-spaced mopane poles, buried deep in the ground and bolted together at the corners, with one pen for each elephant. It had been an expensive mistake, but Leslie was the last elephant we lost.

On that first trial run in 1966, we caught two more young elephants without incident. We had no deaths, injuries or escapes, and no trouble from cows defending their young. After the difficulties we had had with Leslie, we were surprised to see how quickly the young elephants settled down in the stockade, and within a few days of capture they had no fear of man whatsoever (Plate 23). Game Guards and labourers were employed to cut food from the bush, and within two weeks the young elephants could be led out for short walks in the surrounding area to feed by themselves.

The second capture exercise in May 1967 was just as successful, and although we darted and immobilised a total of ten young elephants, only six were retained for export. They were eventually sold for £300 each, and ended up in zoos in Britain, West Germany and America.

It is unfortunate that live capture of elephants can never become a realistic alternative to killing where large numbers of animals must be removed. At best it should be considered as an alternative way of dealing with young elephants which would otherwise have been shot in the course of culling programmes.

4
Age and growth

I am always being asked by interested laymen how long an elephant lives, how you can tell its age, and how big it can grow. This indeed was a vitally important part of my overall research programme, because in any applied population study such as mine it is essential to be able to age individual animals as accurately as possible. Of course an approximate indication of an elephant's age can be obtained from field observations of living animals, by comparing relative shoulder heights, total body lengths, body proportions and tusk growth but these approximations are inadequate for the more precise studies that I required and so I had to base my research on the examination of post-mortem material.

The killing of hundreds of elephants, which I have just described, for the protection of the habitat provided these post-mortem specimens not only in the Luangwa Valley but also elsewhere in the continent, and has presented a unique opportunity for detailed comparative studies of elephant populations throughout their range. It has also led to a refinement of age determination techniques.

The best techniques so far described are related to the replacement and wear of the elephants' molar teeth; but any method of age determination must be checked for accuracy against specimens or animals of known age, and this is a problem; how to obtain specimens necessary for this calibration. There are very few known-age elephants in captivity, and even fewer under natural or semi-natural conditions in Africa itself. What is more those elephants that are held in captivity must be examined with caution. Good feeding and lack of stress could cause precocious development whereas poor diet could cause dental decay. On the whole, animals held in captivity usually grow faster and taller than those in the wild.

An additional complication in age determination studies is the variation between individuals *within* a population. For example, it would be most unlikely for all the animals in one population to have teeth that erupt at exactly the same age or wear down at the same rate. The variation that exists in a class of six-year old children will show just what I mean. Furthermore, there are bound to be differences between males and females, and yet nearly all age determination techniques assume that the sexes are identical. Finally, there is the unknown component of genetic variation *between* populations: can we assume

68

that a technique described for elephants in East Africa will apply with equal reliability to elephants in Zambia or in South Africa?

With this in mind, I set about collecting all the elephant lower jaws I could lay my hands on in the Luangwa, both those from the culling programme and any found in the bush. The latter source yielded very few specimens, and in my final analysis I was virtually restricted to animals from the abattoir.

Lower jaws are comparatively easy to collect, move around and measure, in contrast to the skulls that contain the upper set of teeth, which are unbelievably heavy and difficult to manoeuvre, and as the extraction of the teeth from them is very time-consuming, all the elephant studies I know of have been restricted to lower jaw collections.

We constructed a sturdy fenced enclosure not far from the abattoir, and this housed my specimens. More often than not, fresh ones from the abattoir had small amounts of meat attached, and although we tried to scrape them off, the residual smell and fresh-looking appearance was enough to attract both hyaenas and vultures. The hyaenas broke in once – in spite of our fence – and carried off two big jaws which we never recovered. The vultures came several times. They never succeeded in taking any jaws, but caused chaos in their fights for what few scraps were available, moving and breaking up my carefully regimented lines of jaws that had taken me hours to measure and group into classes.

Before I describe how all these specimens were used, I must outline the unusual dentition of the elephant because this provides the key to age determinations, and in some cases may help to determine the sex as well. The elephant has no canine teeth. The tusks are actually incisors which grow down from the premaxillary bone in the skull. A pair of deciduous tusks (or tushes) are present at birth, but never show externally. These are replaced at about one year of age by the permanent tusks which become visible externally for the first time at about 30 months, providing a simple but useful field guide (Plate 12); indeed this was one of the techniques I used when looking for very young elephants from the helicopter in the Zambezi Valley.

The increase in size and mass of tusks with age has always fascinated man, and elephants with unusually shaped or large tusks have always attracted attention (Plates 7 and 24). In both sexes, tusk growth is continuous throughout life. In females it can be represented by a straight line, with a *mean* combined mass at puberty of about three kilograms increasing to about 18 kilograms by the end of the animal's life-span. In males there is considerable variation in growth patterns, but in all males the rate of growth increases progressively throughout life. The *mean* combined mass of male tusks at puberty is about eight kilograms, but from then on the rate of increase varies tremendously between individuals and localities. Big tusks are the result of prolonged growth, but extremely big tusks probably result not only from prolonged but from unusually rapid growth. Tusks of females grow long and slender while those of males continue to thicken as they lengthen, and this provides a useful guide to the determination of the sex of elephants in the field.

But as much as the tusks fascinate the layman it is the unusual molar teeth of the elephant that form the basis for age determination techniques (Fig. 3). Six molar-like teeth develop on each side of the upper and lower jaw of the elephant

69

Plate 24. Striking or unusual tusk formations readily identify certain elephants.

and for simplicity these have been designated M_1 to M_6. All of the six teeth are deciduous (they are shed during the elephant's life), and at any one time no more than two of the six teeth are in wear simultaneously in any one half of the jaw. Each tooth that comes into wear is longer and wider than the previous one, and this helps identify them (Fig. 4). As each molar comes into wear, it moves forward to the front of the jaw where small fragments get worn down and broken off (Fig. 5 and Plate 25), and the next one grows forward from the back of the jaw to replace it.

In 1966 Dick Laws published a most valuable paper that made use of the elephant's molar replacement in the lower jaw to describe and illustrate 30 age groups, to which he assigned chronological ages. The groups were related to the progressive eruption and wear of the six teeth. Arbitrary estimates were made of the intervals between successive age groups and these were subsequently checked against growth and seasonal ridges on the roots. Comparisons were also made with known-age material. Laws concluded that the six molars were fully developed and erupted (but not worn down) at the following ages:

70

Tooth	Age in years
M_1	1
M_2	2
M_3	6
M_4	15
M_5	28
M_6	47

Eventually the last molar, M_6, is worn down, and Laws estimated that at about 60 years of age just a fragment of the tooth remains.

It is interesting to note that as long ago as 1918, R. I. Pocock exhibited a series of molar teeth of elephants that had died in London Zoo. He described the wear on the last molar (M_6) of a 50-year-old elephant, and reported that about one third of the tooth had been lost. As the tooth had come into wear at about 40 years, Pocock concluded that the elephant would have been toothless before it was 70.

An elephant with a few remaining fragments of M_6 soon dies of starvation, as it is unable to chew its food. In other words, the final wearing down of M_6 places an absolute upper limit of about 60 years to an elephant's life-span. Plate 26 on p.74 shows the large undigested fibres in the droppings of an elephant that Peter Guy came across in his feeding study. Not surprisingly the animal, which died soon after the photograph was taken, had only small fragments of M_6 remaining in both top and bottom jaws.

In 1969 Roger Short provided a useful confirmation of one of Laws' age classes. He described how an elephant called Diksie died in London Zoo at the age of 27 as a result of trauma when she fell into the moat surrounding her enclosure. A film taken by an onlooker at the time of the incident shows that she was in fact pushed by one of the Asiatic elephants. An examination of her teeth revealed that M_5 was in full wear, which corresponds closely with the age

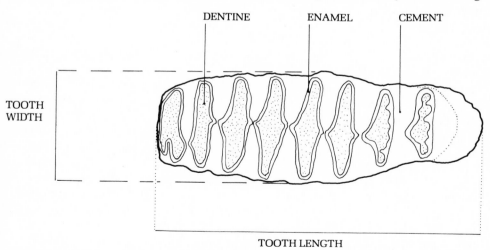

Figure 3. An occlusal view of an elephant's molar tooth, showing the main measurements that are used to identify each of the six teeth. The series of hard enamel ridges, which have a characteristic pattern of lozenge-shaped, or 'loxodont' ridges, are bonded together by cementum.

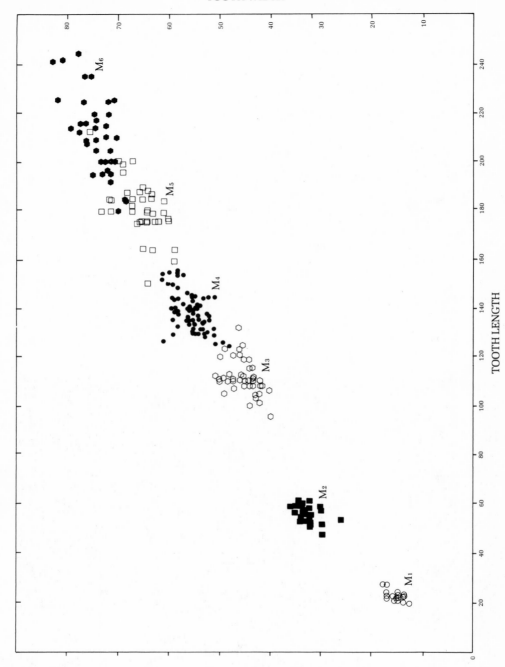

Figure 4. A plot of tooth width (mm) against tooth length (mm) for M_1-M_6, for female elephants from the Luangwa Valley. This progressive increase in length and width facilitates identification of the six molars.

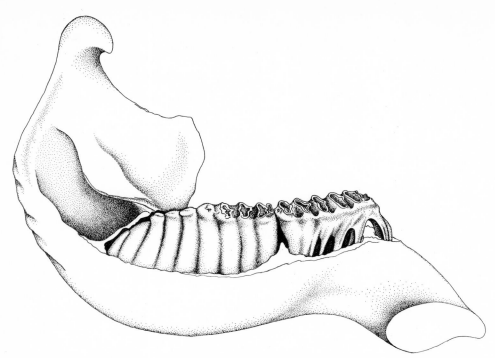

Figure 5. A medial view of the lower jaw of an elephant, showing M_4 replacing M_3.

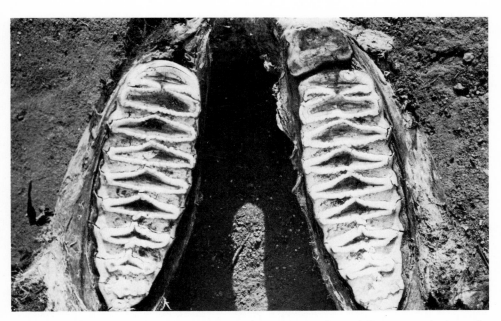

Plate 25. The lower jaw of an elephant, showing the sixth molar almost fully worn. At the front of the right half of the jaw, a fragment of the fifth molar is still present.

Plate 26. These large undigested fibres formed part of the droppings of a 60-year-old elephant. The sixth molar was so worn down that the elephant could no longer chew its food and it died.

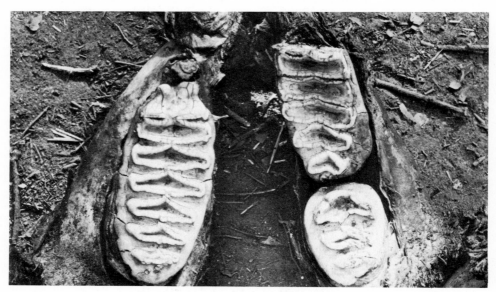

Plate 27. The lower jaw of an elephant with the sixth and last molar well worn. At the back of the right half of the jaw is a rare additional (or supernumerary) molar.

assigned by Laws to that particular stage of molar progression. Diksie's M₅ had extensive dental decay which has never been observed in elephants in the wild. It seems likely that the abnormal zoo diet – including food supplied by members of the public – was the cause.

The age determination technique described by Laws has the advantage of simplicity, and furthermore there has been confirmation of certain of the age classes. As a consequence it has been widely used throughout Africa. Other techniques have been described and are listed in the references to this chapter at the end of this book, but these have not gained wide acceptance.

Laws's 1966 paper was based on a collection of 385 lower jaws from western Uganda, and in his sample four of the jaws had extra (or supernumerary) teeth. I examined 1 236 lower jaws from the elephants killed or found dead in the Luangwa Valley, and only one in the whole collection had a supernumerary tooth, a 53-year-old female with an additional molar in the lower right jaw (Plate 27).

Credit for finding that specimen must go to Carol. We were living in our caravan during our first year at the cropping station in the Luangwa and our camp site on the river bank had no facilities whatsoever. We took on a servant, Jonathon Mwandika, to help us bring in water and firewood, and to assist with the washing. He also helped us build a lavatory in the bush, and he found a big lower jaw of an elephant, which he placed upside down over the deep hole he had dug. This made a comfortable and convenient seat.

I left the camp one morning to spend the day measuring and classifying my collection of elephant lower jaws, and when I returned I told Carol about what I had been doing. Later that afternoon she called me over to look at our 'loo seat', which for curiosity she had turned the right way up. She thought there was something unusual about the teeth, and she was right – the jaw contained the one and only supernumerary molar in 1 236 specimens! It was one of the few elephant lower jaws picked up in the bush, and it had been put to good use in more ways than one.

In another study in East Africa, Laws and Ian Parker reported the presence of severe abscesses of the teeth and bony swellings of the jaws of elephants of all ages. Nearly 10% of the elephants were affected in the Murchison Falls area, and they suggested that these abnormalities were symptomatic of stress. I found no abscesses at all in any of the lower jaws from the Luangwa, but I believe it would be wrong to jump to any conclusions about stress in a population from such an observation.

Before I go on to consider the application of the molar wear and progression technique to determine the age structure of a population of elephants, it is worth mentioning another approach to age determination that appears to work quite well: this involves the use of an elephant's eye. The lens of an eye is what biologists refer to as an 'ectodermal' structure, in that material is continually being added to it throughout life. Because of its unique highly protected position in the body there is little or no wear of the lens and with age it steadily increases in size and mass. The basis of the technique is quite simple: as an elephant grows older, its eye lens becomes heavier, and there is a good relationship between eye lens mass and age.

The lens is removed from the eye and stored in a fixative until it can be weighed. For accurate comparative purposes, each lens is thoroughly dried, and then it is carefully weighed in very dry surroundings to avoid it taking in water. The method works well in the elephant, and although it is not as reliable as the examination of tooth wear and replacement, it is a useful back-up technique in cases of doubt or when the teeth have been lost or damaged.

With a good age determination method at my disposal, I was in a position to establish the age structure of the elephant population in Luangwa, study body growth with age and examine variations in reproduction and mortality within each age class. In fact, a whole new world was opened to me, and I began to come up with some exciting and unexpected results.

The establishment of the age structure of the elephant population from a shot sample was integral to my study. I appreciated the problems here, because I could only do this if the elephants I looked at could be regarded as a true *random* sample of the population as a whole. In all the elephant populations studied throughout Africa, males leave the family units soon after they have reached puberty and join or form bachelor groups.

In the Luangwa Valley, complete family units were killed, but the bachelor herds were not sampled. A similar procedure was followed in several other parts of Africa, and in all these cases as a result the overall population age structure could not be determined. However, these studies do permit a comparison of the age structure of the family units provided the same age determination technique is used.

In 1969, Laws compared the age structure of four different elephant populations in East Africa, and reached a very interesting conclusion: he found that all four populations experience cyclical annual variations in births and early mortality that are related to environmental conditions. His age structures were 'smoothed' so as to eliminate possible inaccuracies in age determination. All four populations showed a series of 'peaks' and 'troughs' with a wave-length of about six to eight years, and considerable amplitude. This was the first time that such a cyclical pattern had been described in African mammals, and quite naturally stimulated tremendous interest.

Using the same techniques, I now compared data I had collected in the Luangwa Valley with the Murchison Falls Park North elephant population described by Laws. The only difference was in the 'base years' – Luangwa was 1969 and Murchison Falls was 1966. The end result was most surprising (Fig. 6). The major and pronounced 'troughs' and 'peaks' in Zambia were very similar to the Murchison Falls elephant population, yet in Zambia there was no indication whatsoever of a correlation between rainfall and cyclical annual variations in births and early mortality (cycles of recruitment), as Fig. 6 shows quite clearly. As it is extremely unlikely that the elephants in Zambia would experience cycles of recruitment exactly three years out of phase with elephants in East Africa and of very similar wave-length and amplitude, it must be concluded that as the two populations were aged by the same method, the 'peaks' and 'troughs' are much more likely to be artefacts caused by slight inaccuracies in the age determination technique. Confirmation of this suggestion has come from Butch Smuts in Kruger National Park. He found that the age structure of the elephants in his area

76

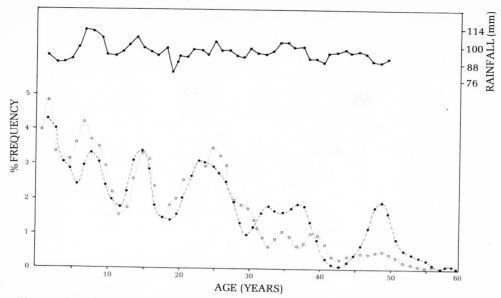

Figure 6. Smoothed three-year running averages of the age structure of the Luangwa Valley elephant family units, base year 1969 (closed circles), compared with the Murchison Falls Park North elephants, sexes combined, base year 1966 (open circles), as described by Laws (1969). The rainfall records are the three-year running averages for the Luangwa Basin, correlated with the 1969 base year.

had peaks and troughs very similar to those from Zambia and East Africa; both 11 and 12-year-olds and 16 and 17-year-olds tended to be under-represented in the Kruger National Park samples.

It must be emphasised that only slight inaccuracies of about two or three years are necessary to produce the apparent cyclical pattern shown in Fig. 6, and in no way does it appear that the general scale of ages assigned by Laws for the elephants is incorrect, especially as known-age elephants have confirmed certain of his classes.

It is perhaps not all that surprising therefore that until large-scale culling operations got underway, there was very little worthwhile information available on the growth rates of elephants because of the difficulties of weighing and measuring a representative sample of animals at different stages of their development. Furthermore, until quite recently no reliable age determination techniques were available.

Some of these difficulties are well illustrated in Viv Wilson's account of his weighing of one bull elephant that he shot in Northern Rhodesia in January 1957. The entire elephant was cut up into small pieces in the field, and everything was weighed, including blood and stomach contents. After several hours' work, with a large team of assistants, he produced the following results:

	Mass in kg
Skin (cut into 42 pieces)	414
Ears (both)	42,5
Trunk (cut into three pieces)	113,5
Shoulder blades (both)	79,5
Tusks (right − 2,1 m long)	37,5
Tusks (left − 1,9 m long)	32
Nerves from tusks (left − 1,2 m long)	5,5
Nerves from tusks (right − 1,4 m long)	6,5
Skull and bottom jaw (excluding brain)	180,5
Penis (1,6 m long)	51
Testicles (20 cm in diameter − both)	5,5
Ribs and spine (cut into 13 pieces)	304
Intestines (excluding stomach contents, fluid, and stomach etc. cut into 31 pieces)	302
Kidneys (weighed in one piece)	8
Heart (weighed in one piece)	25
Liver (cut into four pieces)	77,5
Spleen (as one piece)	18
Lungs (cut into four pieces)	29,5
Tongue (as one piece)	12,5
Tail (cut off at anus)	11,5
Pelvis (with very little meat)	91
Front legs: (1) Bones including foot	77,5
(2) Bones including foot	84,5
Back legs: (1) Bones including foot	72,5
(2) Bones including foot	69
Fluid: (Blood, water, etc. measured in 4 gallon tins at total of 147 gallons = 668 litres)	534,5
Stomach contents: (mainly grass and maize)	539,5
Meat: (mostly red meat cut into 204 pieces)	1 936
Total mass	5 160,5

Almost a full day's work was needed to produce a figure for the total mass of the elephant – a task that I was subsequently able to do in a matter of a few minutes. Nevertheless, Wilson's painstaking approach had the advantage of providing fascinating additional data on the contribution of different parts of the body to the total mass; a study I made no attempt to repeat!

Prior to the Luangwa Valley operation the majority of elephant culling programmes in Africa had not had the opportunity to take the total body mass of whole elephants, especially when the animals are cut up in the field and not returned to a central abattoir. In 1967 Laws, Parker and Archer described a method for estimating the total body mass of an elephant that overcame this problem. They found the dissected hind leg bore a close correlation to the total body mass, and once this relationship had been established for both sexes, the dissected hind leg could be used to predict the total body mass quite accurately. This method is now widely used in many parts of Africa.

78

Why do we go to so much trouble to take all these body measurements? At the outset let me stress that a clear-cut, objective assessment of body growth is much more than just an academic exercise. For example, it is possible that body growth rates slow down in over-utilised habitats where food is scarce, and this in turn could reduce the birth-rate in the population. If this can be determined and measured then it might be possible for a biologist to make more realistic population projections. Growth studies are also essential in the estimation of the population biomass and in the estimation of meat production on a sustained yield basis. Last, but by no means least, information on growth with age is of great value in taxonomic studies and of vital importance in the preparation of field age determination techniques.

The growth in body mass and height with age in male and female elephants in the Luangwa Valley is shown in Figs 7 and 8. (The mathematical derivation of the growth curves is beyond the scope of this book, and I refer the reader to the papers listed for this chapter at the end of the book for further information.)

At birth, both male and female elephants have a shoulder height of about 85 centimetres and a mass of about 120 kilograms, but there are of course exceptions. Butch Smuts recorded two large male foetuses of 144,6 and 164,6 kilograms in the Kruger National Park. At the other extreme was a healthy and very mobile new-born elephant in the Luangwa Valley that had to be killed during a culling operation; it had a mass of a mere 68 kilograms.

By one year of age, the elephants have grown to about 110-115 centimetres and can still just walk below their mothers — as I mentioned earlier, providing a simple field guide to the identification of elephants less than one year old. At

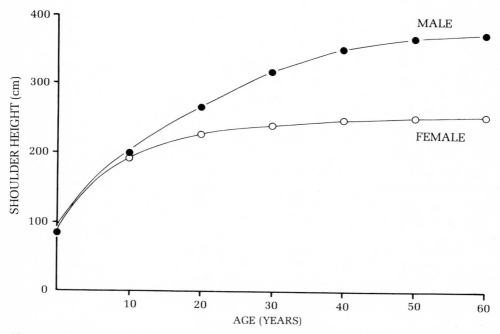

Figure 7. The increase in height with age of male and female elephants in the Luangwa Valley.

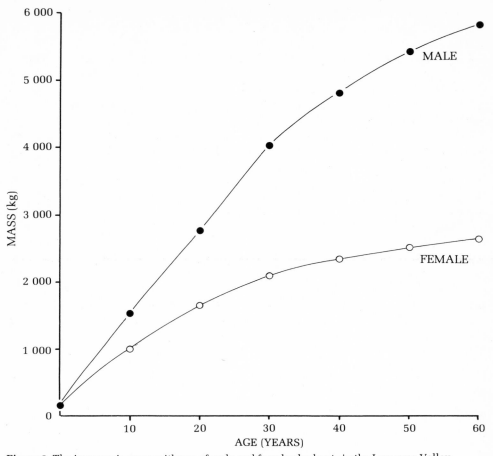

Figure 8. The increase in mass with age of male and female elephants in the Luangwa Valley.

about 30 months the tusks become visible externally and this provides another useful field guide. Once again, there are some notable exceptions. Clive Spinage in 1959 photographed a young elephant that was probably no more than about three years old which had tusks about 30 centimetres long. This was a very exceptional case of precocious tusk growth, and illustrates the importance of using other features such as comparative shoulder height and total body length for field age estimations.

Elephants of both sexes never stop growing (see Figs 7 and 8). The older they get, the taller and heavier they become. The figures also illustrate the difference in growth rates between the sexes, and this underlines the necessity for the correct sexing of elephants in the field when estimating age. The male elephant has no scrotum – the testes are permanently located inside the body cavity – and the penis is often difficult to see when it is not erect (Plate 9). One of the most useful guides to determine the sex of an elephant is the shape of the forehead, which has a peaked appearance in females, but curves smoothly forward and

80

downwards in males (Fig. 9). In addition, males have tusks that are much thicker at the lip-line relative to their length than they are in females.

The group composition should provide the final clue. All the members of a bachelor group will be post-pubertal males, and the absence of young elephants is quite obvious; solitary elephants are almost invariably males (Plate 10). Family units with their complement of adult females and young are unmistakable (Plate 16). With more precise information of the kind shown in Figs 7 and 8 it is now possible to relate the sizes of elephants in family units to that of an average lead cow, and this has been done in Fig. 10. Bulls above about 15 years of age have been excluded (they will have left the family units) and these animals are much more difficult to age in the field. Very often they are solitary, or in small groups of two to four, all much the same age. Hence shoulder height comparisons are not possible, and one has to rely on an examination of tusk circumference and length relative to general body size.

As an approximate guide, tusk circumference at the lip-line doubles between the time the males leave the family units up to about 30 years of age. Over the same period the shoulder height increases by about 100 centimetres. Tusk mass as a basis for age estimation is not too reliable because of the great variations.

A final useful field guide is provided by elephants over about 50 years of age. In these animals the temporal region of the skull (just above the eye), is depressed and sunken, relative to the rest of the skull. This is simply a sign of old age, and is not connected with poor physical condition.

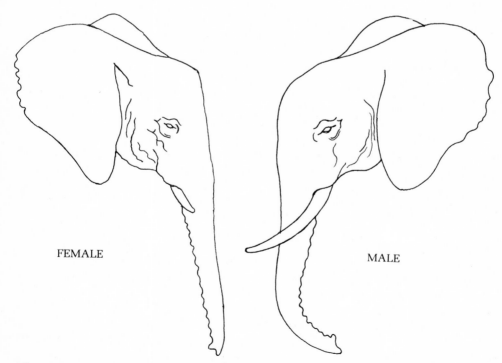

FEMALE   MALE

Figure 9. A comparison of the shape of the forehead in male and female elephants.

81

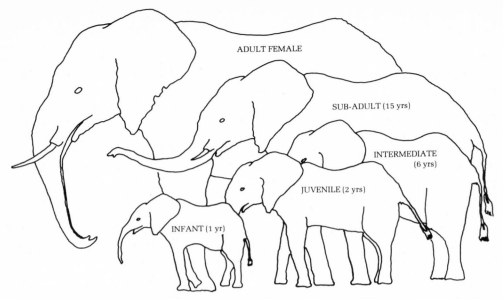

Figure 10. The relative sizes of elephants in a family unit compared with that of an average lead cow. These classifications are useful as preliminary population-structure estimates.

Harvey Croze has tried a new approach to assessing the age of elephants in the field and it appears to have great potential. His technique consists of photographing elephant family units from the vertical position from an aircraft measuring their relative back lengths on the photographs, and then relating the lengths to a mean breeding herd growth curve. The idea should provide a useful supplement to existing field classification methods.

An even more interesting approach to the question is at present being investigated by Anthony Hall-Martin, a Research Officer in Addo Elephant Park, and Heinz Rüther, a Senior Lecturer in the Department of Surveying at the University of Cape Town. The idea originated in a contact with Iain Douglas-Hamilton who had used auxiliary methods based on photogrammetric principles to measure the shoulder height of elephants, the methods being based on the correlation that exists between shoulder height and age. The Department of Surveying at Cape Town expressed an interest in the project, and they pointed out that from a surveyor's point of view the technique used by Douglas-Hamilton could be improved in accuracy and general application. In the current experiments in the Addo project, stereophotography is being employed at ranges varying from five to 80 metres. This requires a special mounting of a pair of very expensive terrestrial surveying cameras on the back of a four-wheel drive vehicle – in case a quick retreat is necessary. Rüther and Hall-Martin hope to perfect and simplify the technique, but already they have measured many of the Addo elephants and their findings are accurate to within one or two centimetres.

If the information contained in the growth curves shown in Figs 7 and 8 had been available earlier this century, much of the confused thinking on the subject of the mysterious pygmy elephant could have been avoided. For example, in

1934 C. E. Brown wrote: 'On April 4, 1925, there arrived at the Philadelphia Zoological Garden a fine specimen of pygmy elephant.' He then gave a series of measurements on which he made the assumption that the specimen was nearly fully grown since the rate of growth had dropped to about two inches (or five centimetres) a year in the last year of measurement (when the elephant was in fact about 12 years old). As it is now known that growth in height falls to five centimetres a year or less by only ten years of age, the elephant described by Brown was certainly not nearly fully grown. We can now say with confidence that the existence of a distinct species of pygmy elephant is entirely unproven.

Before I leave the subject of growth, it is worth recording that the elephant's destruction of the woodland has had a pronounced effect on tusk growth. A comparison of the length of exposed ivory in East African elephants compared with those in Zambia shows that the Zambian tusks are shorter, almost certainly a result of the higher degree of wear in that country as a result of the elephants spending a greater part of their time in woodland debarking trees (Plate 11). The wear caused by this activity must be considerable, and could well mask any real differences in growth in length of tusks between populations.

5
Reproduction

When I moved to the Luangwa Valley in 1968 we had no idea as to why the elephant population had increased in recent years. Here, just as in so many other parts of the continent, people were talking about an 'elephant population explosion', implying that for some reason the numbers had increased, either as a result of a rise in the birth-rate, or a decrease in the death rate, or even a combination of the two.

One of my main tasks was to investigate both these factors, and this led me on to what I believe is the most fascinating aspect of elephant biology: a study of the animals' reproduction, including both behavioural and physiological aspects. In terms of my study, I needed to know to what extent reproductive performance varies with age, season, locality, population density, and plane of nutrition. I then hoped to use this information to predict population growth rates under different environmental conditions.

As an introduction, I must refer back to an earlier study in 1966, when I. O. Buss and J. M. Savidge published a paper on changes in population numbers and reproductive rates of elephants in Uganda. They carried out a series of counts of young elephants under one year of age, these being identified as elephants that could walk under their mothers and had no visible tusks. They concluded that the 'annual increment' in the three populations they studied varied with population density. They recorded an increment of 8% to 9% where the population density was 2,2 elephants per square mile, but in a nearby study area, where the population density had *increased* to 4,5 elephants per square mile the increment had *fallen* to 6-6,5%.

This clearly suggested that some kind of homeostatic or self-regulatory mechanism was at work: as population density went up, the recruitment to the population went down. Their findings created quite a stir: What were the mechanisms involved? Could they be behavioural or nutritional? Was the death rate increasing, or the birth-rate declining, or was it a combination of the two? If the birth-rate had declined, was this due to elephants starting to reproduce later in life, or were they simply reproducing less frequently? These questions were at the forefront of my mind when I started looking at the Luangwa elephants, but before I describe how I studied these various reproductive parameters, let me

84

first give a brief outline of the structure and growth of the elephant's reproductive tract.

The relative positions of the female reproductive organs are shown in Fig. 11. The two ovaries are situated close to the kidneys. The Fallopian tubes are about 30 centimetres long and are quite difficult to see as their junction with the uterine horn is fairly deep in muscular tissue. The uterus has two horns and a common middle but partly divided lumen which leads into a long urogenital passage. This, in turn, opens externally at the vulva. There is a well-developed clitoris. The two mammary glands are situated between the front legs.

Elephant gestation is 22 months – a fact established from a range of observations going back over many years. One of the earliest of these was made by Aristotle, who suggested that gestation was nearly two years; Pliny thought that it was six months! Some really worthwhile observations on the duration of pregnancy were put together from notes collected over a period of more than 40 years from elephant training establishments in the old Belgian Congo. In three carefully observed cases in particular, gestation lasted 22 months, and towards the 16th month of pregnancy the female's mammary glands began to swell visibly. I must emphasise that 22 months is the *average* duration within a recorded range from 17 to 25 months. Many of the older books and journals will tell you that the duration of pregnancy in the elephant varies according to the sex of the foetus, being longer in males than in females, but I am not aware of any evidence to support this. The elephant has the longest known gestation. The record for the shortest goes to an Australian marsupial, the short-nosed ban-

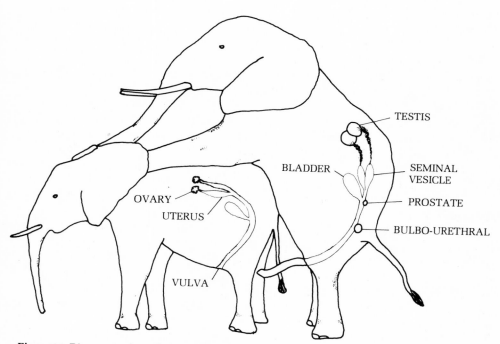

Figure 11. Diagram to show the positions of the male and female reproductive organs (after Short (1972)).

dicoot. Gordon Lyne described this for the first time in 1974 when he observed an interval of 12 days 8 hours and 12 days 11 hours between mating and birth.

It never ceases to surprise people that even when only three months old, an elephant foetus so closely resembles its parents in proportion and shape (Plate 29). How do we know the foetus is only three months old? Taking a mean birth mass of 120 kilograms and a mean gestation period of 22 months, a foetal growth curve can be constructed following a method described by A. St. G. Huggett and W. F. Widdas. This very useful relationship makes it possible to estimate the age of a foetus from its mass, and if the date of collection of the foetus is also known, it becomes possible to estimate its date of conception.

It is inevitable that pregnant elephants are killed when complete family units are being shot, and consequently hundreds of elephant foetuses have been collected throughout Africa in the course of culling operations (Plates 28 and 29). In my work in the Luangwa, I collected a total of 223 foetuses, and all of this material was put to good use. Nobody enjoys killing pregnant females, but as I have already discussed at length earlier it had to be done, and we never wasted the opportunity of getting as much new information as possible from the dead animals. For example, from some of the female foetuses I was able to collect, weigh, and measure foetal ovaries, in this way adding to the information gained from examining hundreds of ovaries from pre- and post-pubertal elephants. As a result of this work I recorded a most pronounced increase in the amount of interstitial tissue in the elephant foetal ovary about half-way through pregnancy, indeed this was so pronounced that the total foetal ovarian mass late in the second half of pregnancy usually exceeded the total mass of ovarian tissue in neonatal and pre-pubertal elephants (Fig. 12) and frequently exceeded the total

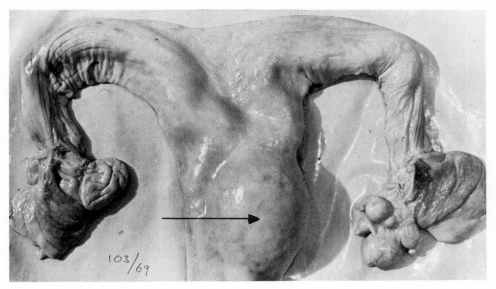

Plate 28. The ovaries and uterus of a 15-year-old elephant. This was the animal's first pregnancy, and the uterus (arrowed) contains a two-month old foetus.

86

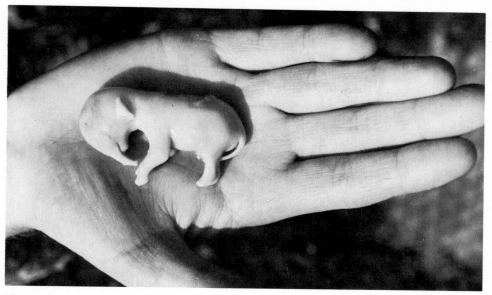

Plate 29. Pregnancy lasts for about 22 months. This foetus is only three months old, but already it has several of the features of a new-born elephant. Growth is very rapid in the second half of pregnancy, and at birth the elephant weighs some 120 kilograms.

mass and the size of the ovaries in post-pubertal animals. I also found that following birth there was a rapid reduction of the mass of the ovaries as a result of a decline in the amount of interstitial tissue, and a pronounced reduction of width relative to length, the ovaries soon assuming the typical pre-pubertal proportions, with ovarian width about one third of ovarian length.

One of my main tasks was to determine the mean age at first ovulation in the elephant population in my study area. To do this, I collected all the ovaries from elephants I could age, and then sliced them longitudinally at about three millimetre intervals and examined them with the naked eye. The females were classified as 'immature' if their ovaries showed no evidence of previous ovulations and 'mature' if at least one ovulation had occurred. Fig. 13 shows the results of an examination of ovaries of elephants up to 22 years of age that I collected in the Luangwa, and I concluded that the mean age at first ovulation was about 14.

My examination of the ovaries also revealed that very few of the elephants were ovulating in the dry season. This was confirmed by relating the month of conception of all the foetuses that were collected to the rainfall pattern (Fig. 14). From 1964 to 1968, 88% of all the conceptions recorded were in the six months from November to April, when nearly all (96%) of the rain fell. It appeared that a change in the elephant's diet from browse and dry grass with its low crude protein content at the end of the dry season, to a diet of fresh green grass with a high protein content at the height of the rains (Table 1), stimulated ovulation and fertile mating. Prior to the post-mortem examination of both ovaries and foetuses, we had no idea that the elephants in Luangwa were seasonal breeders.

87

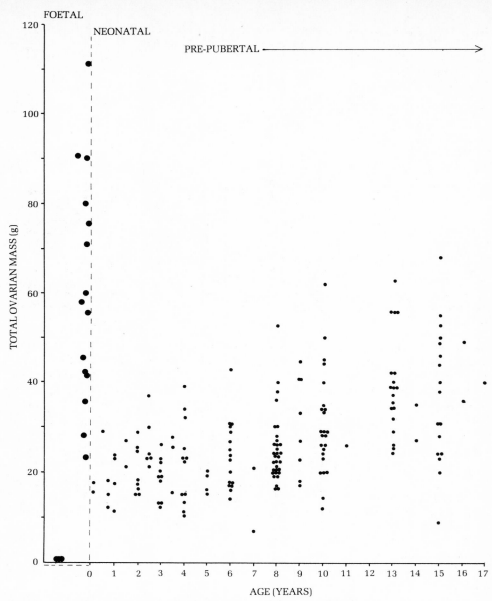

Figure 12. Increase in mass of the foetal, neonatal and pre-pubertal elephant ovary.

Table 1. Crude protein content for natural grassland at Mazabuka in Zambia (From Darling (1960) quoting from an FAO grassland mission to N. Rhodesia).

Month	Crude Protein %	Month	Crude Protein %	Month	Crude Protein %
November	3,35	March	4,6	July	1,08
December	11,01	April	4,3	August	0,86
January	6,13	May	2,2	September	0,68
February	5,15	June	2,1	October	0,64

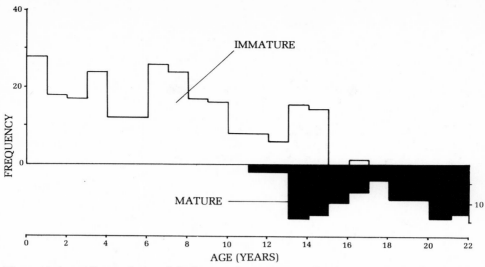

Figure 13. Age at first ovulation of elephants in the Luangwa Valley, based on an examination of their ovaries. *Above* (immature) – no evidence of ovulation. *Below* (mature) – at least one ovulation.

For some unknown reason, in 1969 nearly all of the elephants we examined conceived much later than usual. In fact, the peak occurred well after the height of the rains, and yet the rainy season seemed really no different from that of previous years. It is most unlikely that any nutritional deficiencies should suddenly act together in 1969 to retard breeding and should not do so in previous years. The answer may well lie in the fact that although culling in all the years took place in virtually the same area, there is a possibility that in 1969 a different subpopulation had moved into the area from somewhere else, and it was this subpopulation that was being sampled.

This relationship between timing of conception and rainfall is by no means restricted to Luangwa; it has been found in other parts of Africa, and is usually more pronounced as one moves away from the equator and the rainy seasons

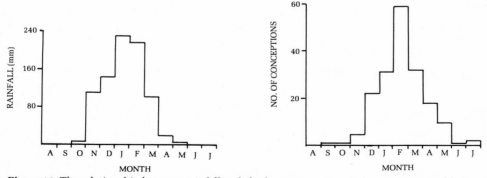

Figure 14. The relationship between rainfall and elephant conception. *Left* – average monthly rainfall from 1963 to 1968 in the Luangwa Valley. *Right* – the monthly frequency of elephant conceptions from 1963 to 1968.

become more distinct. For example, in Kruger National Park, Butch Smuts found that 70% of all conceptions took place in the six months between November to April when 81% of the rain fell, with a lag of one or two months between peak rainfall and peak mating activity.

In all mammals the period from late pregnancy through birth to lactation is a time when mother and offspring are the most vulnerable to extremes of environmental factors, and the elephant is no exception. It would seem logical to suspect that selection would work to fix the mating time so that births would be concentrated in the optimal time of the year. In the Luangwa Valley and in Kruger National Park, the peak of conceptions in the rainy season means that the majority of births takes place 22 months later at the start of the rains, which without doubt is the best time of year from the nutritional point of view.

So far, we have established the age at which elephants start breeding, and the months in which conception occurs. The next factor is the frequency with which elephants give birth, a statistic we refer to as the 'mean calving interval'.

The shot sample I examined provided this information in two different ways. The first method was based on the fact that conceptions occurred in the rains and culling was restricted to the dry season. If there had been a three year calving interval, (and assuming that there was an even distribution of years of conception), in any dry season 66% of the adult post-pubertal elephants sampled would be pregnant. With a four year calving interval 50% would be pregnant, with a five year calving interval it would be 40%, and so on. Fig. 15 shows a theoretical diagram of three different possible elephant calving intervals. The analysis of the Luangwa data on the basis of the above method suggested a mean calving interval of about four years.

The second technique for investigating the frequency with which elephants give birth was first described by Dick Laws in 1967. This method is related to the structure of the elephant's placenta, which has a zonary form (Fig. 16 and Plate 30), and resembles that of the carnivores, the aardvark and the hyrax. At birth, the placental band is about 21 centimetres wide, and a considerable amount of *maternal* tissue from the lining of the uterus comes away with the placental tissue when the afterbirth is shed. This leaves a permanent scar which forms the

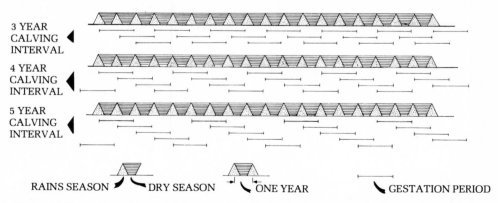

Figure 15. Theoretical diagram of three possible elephant calving intervals. (For explanation, see text).

90

Figure 16. Diagram of the elephant's zonary placenta.

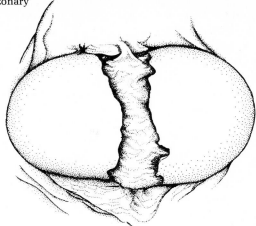

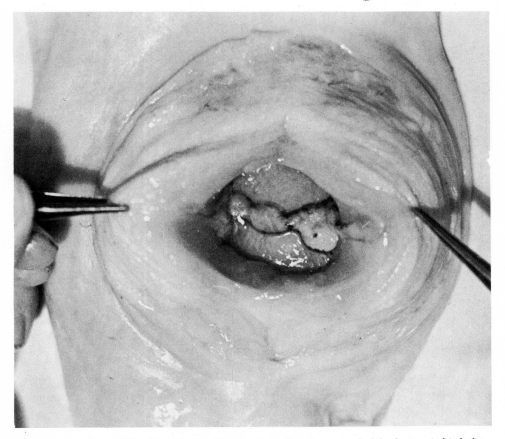

Plate 30. The placental band remains inside the uterus after the removal of the foetus. At birth the placenta is about 21 cm wide, and a considerable amount of maternal tissue from the lining of the uterus comes away with the placental tissue. The resulting scar forms the basis of a technique for estimating the mean calving interval.

basis for this technique for estimating the mean calving interval. In each adult, post-pubertal, non-pregnant elephant, the lining of the uterus is inspected for the presence of these scars, and the number of scars is plotted against the age of the cow. The slope of the line is an estimate of the mean calving interval (Fig. 17) and in the Luangwa population this method gave a mean calving interval of rather less than four years. I will compare these data with those on the frequency of births from other elephant populations in the final chapter.

I never came across a case of twins in any of the 223 pregnant elephants in my study area, although there are now several records from other parts of Africa (see references p.169). In East Africa, for instance, Dick Laws recorded three sets of twins in 222 pregnancies, and in Kruger National Park Butch Smuts recorded two in 353 pregnancies, suggesting that the incidence of twins could be as high as one percent.

A further possible source of variability which interested me was the change in reproductive performance with age, and I have summarised my results in Table 2. In Luangwa there appears to be a peak of fertility in the 18 to 19-year-old elephants, and a reduction from about 40 years. This suggests that reproductive senescence could be related to population density, and thus it could function as another population regulating mechanism. Unfortunately, there is only a limited amount of comparable data from other elephant populations. For example, in the Murchison Falls Park South population in Uganda, Laws found that all the females in the 56 to 60-year-old group were reproductively inactive, and he likened this decline in activity to the human menopause. In contrast, Smuts examined 42 cows over 50 years of age in Kruger National Park and found that 88,1% were either pregnant, lactating or both pregnant and lactating. His sample

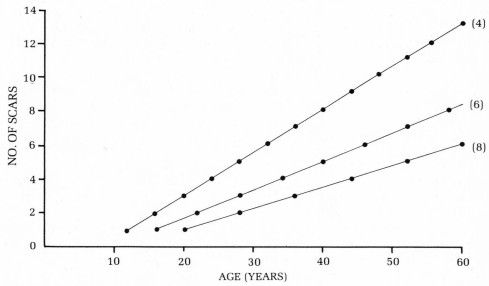

Figure 17. A comparison of three calving intervals (4, 6 & 8 years), based on placental scar counts plotted against age. With the 4 year calving interval, the average age of the first birth was 12 years, with the 6 year calving interval 16 years, and with the 8 year calving interval 20 years.

92

included one 60-year-old cow with a 19-month-old foetus. She was not lactating, and all that was left of M_6 on both sides of the lower jaw were the last two enamel loops.

Table 2. Variations in reproductive performance with age in female elephants from 12 to 60 years of age examined in the Luangwa Valley.

Age (years)	% pregnant	% not pregnant nor lactating (mature females only)
11-12	0	0
13-14	10,3	0
15-17	43,1	0
18-19	76,0	0
20-29	50,6	0
30-39	50,0	0,8
40-49	42,1	6,2
50-60	33,3	16,6

In women menopause imposes an absolute limit to reproductive life when there are no more oocytes available for ovulation. However, in laboratory animals defects in the uterus seem to be the main cause for the decline in fertility associated with advancing age. Perhaps in the elephant, unlike the human female, reproductive senescence may be a combination of uterine defects and a reduction of oocyte number – a possibility which still needs further study.

Before continuing to examine reproduction in the female elephant, in particular the oestrous cycle, we must turn our attention to the male. Aristotle was one of the first to record the variable position of the testes in mammals and he described the permanent intra-abdominal position of the testes in whales and elephants. In the male foetus, and pre-pubertal and adult elephant, the testes are located within the body cavity, and are suspended from the dorsal body-wall very close to the kidneys. Fig. 11 shows the main parts of the reproductive tract in the male.

In mammals with a scrotum, the testes are kept below body temperature when in the scrotal sac, and spermatozoa are stored in a discrete epididymis immediately on top of each testis. But the elephant cannot cool his testes in this way and since its mean body temperature is about 37 °C, this suggests that the whole process of spermatozoa production in the elephant must be particularly temperature-resistant. Furthermore, the elephant has no epididymis. In place of it, a long and highly convoluted duct connects each testis to the opening of the seminal vesicles, and this duct performs the main function of the epididymis of the scrotal mammal – namely the transport, concentration, maturation and storage of the spermatozoa.

Fig. 11 also illustrates why the male elephant requires such a proportionately long and unusually shaped penis. The vagina of the female is ventrally situated, and the male has to hook the end of his penis into it. To do this, the penis has two large dorsally situated levator penis muscles which unite to form a thick common tendon which in turn inserts on the top of the penis near the tip. These muscles account for the characteristic 'S'-shaped flexure of the penis at erection (Plate 31 and Fig. 11), and enables the male to hook the tip of his penis in the

Plate 31. During oestrus, a cow may be mated by several different bulls and coitus itself usually takes less than a minute. The length of the oestrous cycle has still to be determined.

vagina. The length of the penis that enters the vagina is probably rather limited, and if spermatozoa are to reach the uterus, which is still about 60 centimetres away, a large ejaculate volume is required. This in turn accounts for the very well-developed accessory organs of the male. One 20-year-old bull elephant I examined in the Luangwa contained 840 millilitres of fluid in the seminal vesicles, and it is probable that a normal ejaculate is in the region of one litre.

As in the foetal ovary, there is an increase in size of the interstitial tissue in the foetal testis in the second half of pregnancy, with a rapid reduction just after birth. Male elephants in my study were classified as 'mature' if their testes showed some signs of production of spermatozoa and 'immature' if they did not.

It must be emphasised at this point that although an animal may be classified as mature on the basis of the production of spermatozoa it does not necessarily follow that the same animal will mate with females, as the older males tend to keep the younger males away.

I found that the mean age of the start of spermatozoa production was about 15, when the combined testes mass reached 650 to 700 grams. Recent comparative studies in other parts of Africa have indicated that in most elephant populations, male and female elephants reach maturity at about the same age. In other words, when females ovulate for the first time, males of about the same age have just started the production of spermatozoa and at this age they leave the family units to join or form bachelor herds.

Although it is quite clear that females are seasonal breeders, there is as yet no positive evidence for cyclical reproductive activity in the male. The testis continues to grow throughout life, and in normal bulls over 40 years of age each testis will weigh over 3 000 grams.

There is a great deal of confusion surrounding the phenomenon of 'musth'. The term arose in connection with domesticated male Asiatic elephants. It is a time when the adult bulls become aggressive and very dangerous – they may even try to kill their mahouts. Recent studies by M. R. Jainudeen and others have shown that musth occurs once a year in all adult male Asiatic elephants at a time when the male hormone testosterone is at a very high level.

Just before musth starts, the temporal gland (which is situated on the side of the head and opens onto the surface of the cheek between the eye and the ear by means of a single small duct) starts to secrete, and discharges a strong-smelling watery secretion down the side of the face. Only an occasional temporal discharge has been reported in the female Asiatic elephant.

African elephants also have temporal glands, often incorrectly described as musth glands, but here they are active in nearly all age groups of *both sexes* (Plate 16). I must stress that no relationship has been found between the activity of the temporal gland and reproductive status of the African elephant, and the term 'musth' should be restricted to the post-pubertal male Asiatic elephants, where it is characterised by aggressive behaviour and a discharging temporal gland. The possible function of the temporal gland in the African elephant is something I will discuss later.

In 1966 Roger Short published an account of an African elephant he had observed in the field throughout most of its three-day period of oestrus during which the cow was mated by many different bulls. Initially there was little competition between the bulls for the cow, but as oestrus wore on, fighting broke out amongst the bulls and one eventually established dominance, driving the others away. This bull showed no discharge from its temporal gland.

Mating itself took less than one minute on every occasion. Yet, in spite of such observations, we still do not know the length of the oestrous cycle in the African elephant. It is probably about three weeks, the same as in its Asiatic counterpart.

The ovaries provide a fascinating study in themselves because of the amazing variation in the number of ovulations that occur in the elephant before each pregnancy (I found from two to 26 in the elephants I examined). Furthermore, the *corpora lutea* vary tremendously in size and shape (Plate 32). (The *corpus luteum* is a yellow glandular structure that replaces the ovum in the ovary – it secretes a hormone, progesterone, which is essential for the maintenance of pregnancy.)

In a study I did with Roger Short, we found that the elephant can be either monovular or polyovular, and that ovulation is spontaneous. There is no evidence for ovulation during pregnancy. Elephants appear to be unique in their reproductive inefficiency in that they seem to need to ovulate several times in order to accumulate a certain critical mass of luteal tissue in their ovaries before a

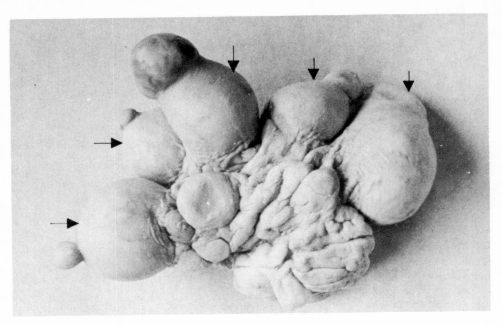

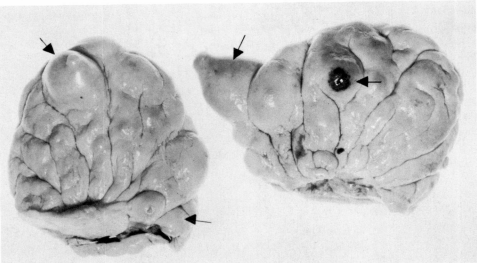

Plate 32. Ovaries of the elephant, with arrows pointing to recent ovulation sites. There is an astonishing variation in the number of ovulations that occur in the elephants before each pregnancy and consequently corpora lutea vary tremendously in size and shape.

pregnancy will follow. The *corpora lutea* appear to be extremely inactive, and very little progesterone is secreted by them compared with other mammals. If progesterone is necessary for pregnancy, then the elephant must be extremely sensitive to it.

Three stages of the reproductive process remain for us to consider in order to complete this chapter; they are birth, lactation and weaning.

Very few people have been lucky enough to witness the birth of an African elephant in the wild, but Walter and Barbara Leuthold are a notable exception. Not only did they witness a birth, but they also took some outstanding photographs (see sequence on pages 98-103). It took place in the Samburu Game Reserve in Kenya, where they came across a group of 12 elephants feeding amongst *Acacia* trees lining the Uaso Nyiro River. Among them they noticed one cow which kept walking backwards and bending her hind legs as if to squat or sit down. Then, without any further warning, there was a tremendous commotion, with loud rumblings, growling and trumpeting, and the Leutholds were amazed to see a new-born baby elephant lying in the short grass. Still completely enveloped in the foetal membranes, it was struggling weakly with its limbs.

Birth must have taken place very quickly. The other elephants gathered around the baby, extending trunks in its direction and showing all signs of excitement, but apart from the mother (the cow that had been walking backwards) only the largest cow in the group approached the baby closely. The mother immediately began to 'peel off' the foetal membranes from the new-born elephant with her trunk, tusks and forefoot. When the membranes were removed she nudged the baby continuously, once even pulling it up from the ground by holding it between her trunk and tusks. She seemed to want to get it on its feet as soon as possible, and 20 minutes after birth the baby stood on its own for a few seconds before falling over.

Gradually its efforts to stand up on its own became more successful and the mother turned her attention to the foetal membranes lying on the sand nearby, grabbing part of them with her trunk and waving this about in the air. Eventually she ate several pieces, but not all of it. At one point another cow picked up a piece of membrane and started swinging it about as well, but she soon dropped it. For a time, the mother and two other cows scraped the ground vigorously with their forefeet, an action that the Leutholds suggested could be interpreted as 'burying' the membranes, although the elephants did not cover them completely.

By now, the new-born elephant was searching for its mother's mammary glands, and about 30 minutes after birth it succeeded for the first time in suckling for one or two minutes. The other elephants gradually lost interest, and moved off to continue feeding, leaving one small adult cow and a young five to six year old male with the mother and baby. This group of four elephants remained together, and about an hour after birth took the baby into their midst and moved off slowly to the *Acacia* trees.

In the wild, suckling continues for at least two years, the young elephant turning its trunk up and slightly back to suck with its mouth (Plate 45). It is usually weaned when it is two years old, especially if the calving interval is four years, but it may occasionally suckle even after the birth of the next calf. Weaning may be delayed if the calving interval is longer.

By observing domesticated elephants at Gangala Na Bodia in the Congo, H. H. Roth obtained positive evidence that foster mothers will adopt and suckle orphan calves. However, there do not appear to be any observations anywhere in Africa of suckling calves moving around from cow to cow within a family unit.

This is the extraordinary sequence of photographs taken by Barbara and Walter Leuthold who witnessed the birth of a calf.

Plate 33. Amidst a group of elephants feeding on the banks of the Uaso Nyiro River, they noticed one of the cows acting unusually. She kept walking backwards, bending her hind legs as if to squat.

Plate 34. Suddenly there was a tremendous commotion of loud rumblings, growlings, trumpeting – and a new-born calf, still enveloped in the foetal membranes, appeared in the short grass.

Plates 35, 37. The mother immediately began to peel off these membranes with her trunk, tusks and forefeet.
36. The other elephants milled around but only the lead cow approached mother and child closely.

Plates 38-41. As the membranes came off, the mother made every effort to get the baby on its feet as soon as possible, nudging it continuously. Once she even dragged the weakly struggling calf up from the ground using her trunk and tusks. Twenty minutes after birth, the baby stood on its own for a few seconds before falling over.

Plate 42. Once the infant could stand, the mother turned her attention to the discarded membranes. She grabbed and waved them about in the air and finally ate several fragments.

Plate 43. The new-born calf began searching for the mammary glands (clearly visible between the mother's front legs) and after about half an hour of life, it succeeded in suckling for the first time for one or two minutes.

Plate 44. An hour after the birth, the now enlarged family unit moves off into the woodland.

Many people cannot believe that the hyrax, or dassie, is related to the elephant, and I am often asked if I believe it is true. I do and, because much of the evidence involves reproductive features, let me digress for a moment to discuss this unexpected relationship. The initial credit for the idea must go to G. G. Simpson who suggested the creation of a super-order of mammals called *Paenungulata* containing three mammalian orders: Hyracoidea (the hyrax), Proboscidea (the elephant), and Sirenia (the sea cows). He based this on the fossil record, because all three orders could be traced back to common Eocene fossil forms in Egypt. The fossil history shows that the hyrax became separated from the elephants and the sea cows at a very early stage in evolution. The evolutionary trend in the hyrax was for a decrease in size, while the elephant took the opposite evolutionary path to attain mammoth dimensions. Although the modern hyrax and elephant seem so very different, they do nevertheless have several features in common that involve aspects of the skeleton and also the reproductive anatomy and physiology in the male and female.

First of all, the structure of the toes is very similar; all four are present and quite close together in both the hyrax and the elephant. We can contrast this with the one prominent toe in the zebra, the two toes of the antelope, and the three of the rhino. Both the elephant and the hyrax have a well-developed pair of upper incisors, and they have various bones in the skull that are similar in structure and position.

The reproductive features are particularly interesting. Both species are members of the *Testiconda* – a small group of mammals that has no scrotum and in

Plate 45. In the wild, suckling continues for at least two years. The young elephant turns its trunk up and slightly back and sucks with its mouth.

which the testes are permanently situated inside the body cavity. In addition, there are a number of important features in common that involve the anatomy and microscopic structure of the ducts responsible for carrying the spermatozoa from the testes to the penis.

The females share three main reproductive features. The structure of the placenta and foetal membranes is very similar in both the hyrax and the elephant, and quite unlike that found in most other mammals. Secondly the hormone that maintains pregnancy – progesterone – is present in extremely small quantities in both species, again quite unexpected and quite unlike any other mammals. Finally both species have relatively long gestation periods – 22 months in the elephant, and seven and a half months in the hyrax – and they both produce precocious young. It is entirely possible that this surprisingly long gestation period of the hyrax is an evolutionary vestige from the times when the ancestral forms were much larger.

I am convinced that most of these reproductive features are important factors pointing to a common ancestry of the hyrax and the elephant for the simple reason that they have remained relatively unchanged during the evolution of mammals presumably because of their comparatively protected position in

104

which they are isolated from the selective effects of the external environment, and the conservative nature of these features has, I believe, made them of great value in considering possible evolutionary relationships.

Now that we have seen the way in which elephants reproduce and how the various reproductive parameters of importance can be measured it is vital, in terms of the elephant problem, to know the overall rate of elephant population increase in each area. Excluding immigration and emigration, this is determined by the birth-rate minus the death rate, and so it follows that the next aspect of elephant biology to consider is mortality.

6
Mortality

Although a great deal of very useful information has been collected in different parts of Africa on all aspects of elephant reproduction, unfortunately the same cannot be said for elephant mortality. Indeed as we shall see in the final chapter of this book, variations in mortality, especially neonatal mortality, are far more important in determining the rate of population growth than are variations in reproductive performance. Yet here is one vitally important field of elephant biology where we are desperately short of good data.

We are only just beginning to understand and determine some of the factors that are responsible for the death of elephants, but the actual quantification of this mortality leaves a great deal to be desired. For convenience I group these factors under the headings: predation (excluding man), disease and parasites, accidents, drought, starvation, stress, hunting and poaching, old age and fighting.

Records of predation on elephants by carnivores are few and far between. In 1945 Pitman reported that 'young elephants are not infrequently killed by lions in Uganda' but made no estimate of the numbers involved. C. D. Trimmer, again in Uganda, witnessed an adult lioness, accompanied by two cubs, trying to seize an elephant calf, but she was killed by a thorax wound from an elephant's tusk. Pienaar had no reliable records of predation on elephants in Kruger National Park, but reported an observation from the Luangwa Valley where 'an elephant of about five feet high and with tusks nine inches long, was the victim of lions'. The calf was first hamstrung and then killed by a bite in the lower part of the throat.

There is no doubt that elephant meat is quite acceptable to the predators. There are several records of hyaenas eating dead elephants, and in 1967, when I was flying in a helicopter in the Zambezi Valley, I saw a lion eating an elephant that had been shot the day before. With so few positive records of predation, it seems reasonable to conclude that the predators of Africa have not played a significant rôle in limiting elephant populations.

The rôle of disease and parasites in the elephant is rather more difficult to assess. Under natural conditions, all free-living wild animals harbour their own, very often specific species of parasites. These rarely reach levels that cause clinical parasitism, but when the animal suffers from poor nutrition or behavioural stress, it is quite possible that internal parasites could become a serious problem.

In Rhodesia, John Condy has made a detailed study of the ten genera of internal parasites found in local elephant populations; he suggests that the monitoring of levels of parasites in animals could be a useful guide to assessing whether or not a species is overpopulated in a given area. Condy pointed out that in some of the more seriously overcrowded national parks, the plane of nutrition of several of the elephants had been lowered. In these restricted areas, the greater density of animals could lead to a heavier contamination of the environment and ultimately result in heavier worm burdens, further endangering the survival of the host species.

In the summer months in Rhodesia it is hot and wet and much of the elephant's diet is grass. Dung beetles break down the elephant droppings rapidly, exposing a greater surface area to the sun and accelerating desiccation of infective nematode larvae. In other words, in the summer months the percentage survival of the infective larvae is reduced. In contrast, in the dry months, most of the elephant's diet is browse, but this is *not* a source of the infective nematode larvae; the waterholes are the culprit. In the dry months the elephants concentrate to drink at a few waterholes which are contaminated by faeces and these are probably the main source of infestation. Condy suggests that, as many of the watering points are already artificial, raising the water into tanks one metre above the ground would present no real problems, and would lessen faecal contamination considerably.

Sylvia Sikes also made a thorough and comprehensive review of elephant parasites, as well as infectious and contagious diseases. She concluded that there was no evidence that parasites were debilitating whole wild elephant populations. Nevertheless, in spite of her conclusions, the disturbing fact remains that the wildlife sanctuaries of Africa are becoming very artificial and more and more isolated from one another as each day goes by; this in turn lends support to Condy's suggestion that parasite levels should be monitored continuously.

An observation of great interest to the medical world came from the research of K. G. McCullagh and M. C. Lewis. In 1967 they published a paper in the *Lancet* in which they described spontaneous arteriosclerosis in the wild African elephant. The lesions they described were essentially similar to those found in man, and yet elephants are herbivores, feeding on a diet containing no animal fats and probably only small amounts of vegetable oils. Sylvia Sikes also studied cardiovascular disease in the African elephant, but in even more detail, and concluded that it was *not* found in elephant populations living in balance with their food resources, but *was* correlated with habitat degeneration associated with overpopulation.

Where there was degeneration of habitat, Sikes described the potential stress factors as excessive continous exposure to sunlight, dietary changes, frustration of the migratory habit, disrupted calving patterns, and overpopulation. She also found that cardiovascular disease was not related to age, a finding in marked contrast to my own observations in Zambia (and later in Rhodesia) and those of

107

Plates 46-49. In Uganda, Erich Wiedemann came across a small elephant entirely bogged down in a mud hole. With the help of a group of local people, he managed to get a rope around it, but when they tried to pull the animal out, it almost submerged.

Plates 50-52. After much effort, the abandoned elephant was pulled clear, and pushed onto its feet. It was frightened and exhausted, but later wandered off.

J. S. Dillman and W. R. Carr in the Luangwa Valley in particular. We found that the arteriosclerotic lesions increased in number and in calcification with age, particularly in female elephants. In fact, in most cases I could age an elephant to within ten years simply by looking at its dorsal aorta! Furthermore, there was no evidence that even the elephants with the heaviest arteriosclerotic lesions showed a loss of condition.

McCullagh published another paper on arteriosclerosis in the African elephant in 1972 and this confirmed that the extent of the disease in the aorta was dependent on age. He also suggested that it was primarily a repair reaction to haemodynamic damage, and reached the important conclusion (as far as the population biologist is concerned) that death from occlusion of the main coronary arteries must be extremely rare in the wild elephant.

There is increasing evidence to suggest that accidents of various kinds can cause the death of a considerable number of elephants each year, in particular the younger animals. R. M. Bere went as far as saying that rarely do more than two calves out of three survive their first year, and that all young elephants are vulnerable to lion, hyaena and snake-bite. He also noted that drowning, getting stuck in deep mud, and being crushed to death by falling trees or older elephants are among known calamities. In his book *Elephants in Africa,* F. Melland describes how five elephants became 'bogged in the swamps by the exit of the Luapula from Lake Bangweulu (N. Rhodesia). They had sunk up to their middles and were slowly going down inch by inch. They could not move and were piteously terrified.'

It is reasonable to expect that young elephants will have far greater difficulties with rivers in flood and with swamps than the adults. Norman Carr once saw the carcass of a young elephant being swept down one of the rivers in Zambia, and he was assured by reliable local witnesses that this often happened.

In Uganda, Erich Wiedemann came across a small elephant entirely bogged down in a mud hole (Plate 46). With a group of local people, he managed to get a rope around the elephant, but it almost submerged when they tried to pull it out (Plates 47-49). Eventually they made long levers from branches of trees and were able to pull the elephant clear. It was frightened and exhausted, but later recovered and wandered off (Plates 50-52).

Wiedemann's elephant was about three or four years old, and elephants of that age are very strong and active, as we had found out to our cost in our initial attempts to catch young Leslie in the Zambezi Valley! If animals of that age could get stuck in the mud, then it is hardly surprising that the much younger ones do so too.

In 1973 I came across a similar situation in Wankie National Park. We had left Zambia by then and I was lecturing at the University of Rhodesia. I was also involved in presenting a wildlife programme called 'Untamed Rhodesia' for Rhodesia Television and we were visiting Wankie to get some original film on the impact elephants were having on the vegetation surrounding the waterholes. Stopping on the edge of a pan in the middle of the afternoon I noticed a very young elephant stuck in the mud but with a bit of a struggle it managed to pull itself clear and came out and stood next to me. Frank Thomas, the RTV camera-man, rushed down to join me at the water's edge and started filming as quickly as he could. I estimated that the calf was no more than a few weeks old. There were no other elephants anywhere in sight, and the miserable creature followed me around wherever I went. As darkness fell, we had to return to camp, leaving the elephant where it was, on its own. Frank Thomas managed to get nearly 30 minutes of excellent film which was finally edited down to just under ten minutes. It was a pathetic and yet at the same time quite moving sequence. I presented the film and story at the end of one programme, concluding by saying that we really had no alternative but to leave the animal where it was: elephants of that age are almost impossible to bring up in captivity, and the animal's best chance for survival was to leave it at the pan in the hope that its mother would return that night. When the programme went on the air we received several very

Plate 53. The huge fan-like ears of the African elephant are one of its most distinctive features. When the elephant assumes a defensive posture, or attacks intruders, the ears are held at right angles to the body and such posturing effectively enlarges its general appearance.

112

irate telephone calls, and all those who 'phoned wanted to know how I could possibly be so heartless towards such a poor, defenceless animal!

In the next programme the following week I went on to tell what actually happened. Two African Game Guards who were camped nearby reported that during the night a herd of elephants came down to drink. The abandoned calf joined up with them and by morning all had disappeared back into the bush. We had made the right decision and I was forgiven! We never did discover why the young elephant had been abandoned. Its mother might have died soon after it was born, and it could have been adopted by another cow. In a case like that, I should imagine that the 'maternal bond' would not be all that well-developed. An alternative suggestion is that the abandoned calf's mother was very young and inexperienced. This might have been her first offspring, and if her family unit had been drinking at the pan and had been suddenly disturbed, she could well have panicked and rushed off leaving her new calf behind. We will never know.

There is a growing body of evidence that drought could be one of the most important factors controlling elephant populations in Africa. As drought in its turn restricts plant growth, drought and starvation go hand in hand as mortality factors. I witnessed a case of drought *on its own* causing the death of elephants in the Siloana Plains in the Western Province of Zambia in October 1970. In 1969/1970, the rainfall for the area had been well below average, and when I arrived there in October there was only one pool remaining. A flight over the

Plate 54. When elephants lose condition, the backbone becomes very prominent, and the pelvic girdle sticks out above the body contours.

plains revealed 31 elephant carcasses within a two kilometre radius of this one pool, and I was able to locate and age 13 of these animals. One elephant was 55 years old, and the remainder were less than four years old, typical of a stress situation in which the very young and very old are the first to die. During my visit to the pool, I saw several elephants in extremely poor condition – some of them could hardly walk. One of these very sick animals was so close to death, that we shot it. I carried out a post-mortem examination which revealed that the contents of the stomach and intestine were abnormally dry, and it was clear that while the elephant had been consuming large quantities of mud, it had eaten little in the way of vegetation. The majority of the elephant droppings nearby were composed of dry mud surrounding a few fragments of grass and mopane leaves. There can be no doubt that drought was responsible for the death of these elephants. Staff of the Department of Tsetse Control who were working in the area estimated that there were about 200 elephant carcasses at or near dried-up waterholes at other localities in the Siloana Plains, and they reported several cases of elephants eating mud, probably in an attempt to extract some water. The one remaining pool had sufficient water in it to support all the elephants in the area, yet only a few elephants had found it. Even more surprising was the fact that the Zambezi River was no more than half a day's walk away, and there was nothing preventing the elephants moving there.

The elephants pictured in Plate 54 are typical of animals in very poor condition. Peter Albl, one of the vets working at the abattoir, who made a study of how to assess the physical condition of elephants, noticed that tremendous individual variations of external anatomical features complicated his work because many of these features were more age- than condition-dependent. He concluded that the external features that best indicate elephants in poor condition are a pronounced lumbar depression and a prominent lateral wing of the ilium on the pelvic girdle. These show up clearly on the nearest elephant in Plate 54. (More recently Bob Malpas has given a very detailed account of the best post-mortem features to use in assessing elephant condition.)

Wankie National Park also experienced an elephant die-off rather similar to that of the Siloana Plains. In 1968 there was a very heavy concentration of elephants around available watering points, and competition for food resulted in some herds moving up to 24 kilometres away from water each day. The competition for water was also acute, particularly where water came from seeps. It was here that most of the deaths occurred. Basil Williamson described how the younger elephants with the shorter trunks were unable to reach the water at the bottom of the holes, and some of these died of thirst. Others were killed by impatient adults in the pushing and shoving that took place around the limited water supplies. Williamson recorded a total of 96 carcasses within one kilometre of water at six different seeps.

The most spectacular documented die-off of recent times occurred in Tsavo Park in the dry years of 1970 and 1971 and many of the deaths were due to

Overleaf: **Plate 55.** In most cases, an elephant's need of sodium can be satisfied in the intake of drinking water. If this is inadequate, however, the elephants will eat soil that has a high concentration of water-soluble sodium.

starvation. Timothy Corfield estimated that about 5 900 elephants died; he determined that there had been a prolonged phase of high juvenile mortality, raised overall mortality and preferential adult female mortality. He suggested that part of the explanation for the higher female mortality could lie with the elephant's social behaviour. As the mother-calf bond is a strong one, adult females would be limited in their search for food to the distances the youngest members of the social group could travel. Elephants usually drink at least once every 24 hours, perhaps even more frequently under very hot and dry conditions (Plates 17 and 19). With severely restricted water supplies, elephants – particularly family units with calves – overutilise the vegetation around the remaining water so that the food supply in these areas becomes progressively poorer. The search for food therefore becomes even more arduous, and under these conditions the youngest elephants collapse and die. Corfield suggested that in these cases the females tied to their calves, became irretrievably weakened and died as well. On the other hand the adult males with their greater independence were perhaps freer of family constraints and were less affected by the harsh conditions.

In recent years there has been speculation that elephant mortality has increased as a consequence of physiological disturbances induced by social pressures related to overcrowding. To examine this proposition there have been various attempts to detect stress by comparative studies of relative adrenal weights in different elephant populations. The adrenals were chosen because studies on other species have shown that an enlargement of the cells of the adrenal cortex is an indication of active defence against damage, a factor which becomes apparent very soon after the application of the stress. Changes in the mass of the adrenal gland provide a suitable indicator of changes in the size of the cortex. In other words, overcrowding, and the associated stress that goes with it, should show up by an increase in relative adrenal mass.

The adrenals of the elephant are elongate structures, flattened dorso-ventrally and situated on the dorsal abdominal wall slightly in front of the kidneys. There is a linear relationship between adrenal mass and age, the adrenals increasing in size by about 7,5 grams per year in both sexes (Fig. 18). This presents obvious difficulties when it comes to making comparisons between elephant populations because the adrenal mass in each sample will be influenced by the age of the elephants to a very great extent. Ideally, for comparative purposes, it would be best to compare the growth in adrenal mass with age in elephant populations in the normal and stressed situations. In the event of stress, if the adrenal cortex has increased in size significantly, this should be detected by an upward displacement of the line shown in Fig. 18. Although a few such studies have been conducted in different elephant populations, as far as I know nobody has yet demonstrated an increase in adrenal mass in the stressed situation. One of the reasons for this could be that there is a lack of good comparative data, simply because the adrenals are quite difficult to find and dissect out intact, in spite of their size. This is certainly an aspect of elephant physiology worthy of further investigation.

The two remaining 'natural' elephant mortality factors are old age and fighting. Nowadays, because of the pressures of hunting and poaching, very few

118

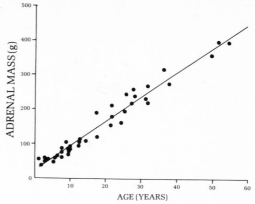

Figure 18. Increase in mass of the adrenals with age in female elephants in the Luangwa Valley. The adrenals increase in mass by about 7,5 g per year. Under stress, it is possible that an upward displacement of the line would occur.

elephants die of old age. Earlier on I described how one elephant died when M₆, the last molar, became too worn down for the animal to chew its food – probably one of the main causes of death in the few elephants that do reach 60 years of age.

Records of elephants dying in fights with one another are very few and far between (Plate 20). One notable exception is an account of a most spectacular battle between two bulls in Wankie National Park in Rhodesia. It was recorded by Ted Davison, and although he did not see the fight itself, he came across the carcass of the defeated animal some days afterwards. The signs of the struggle were obvious from the position of the spoor and from the extensive damage to vegetation. Davison examined the dead elephant and came to the conclusion that the victor had got a tusk into its adversary's mouth and with a sharp upward thrust had broken through to the brain.

There is no doubt, however, that the number of elephants that have died from natural causes in Africa in the last 200 years or so pales into insignificance when compared with the number that have been killed at the hands of hunters and poachers over the same period. It is almost impossible to obtain estimates, but the following few examples are an indication of the scale of the slaughter. Southern and Central Africa have the worst records.

In 1652 elephants occurred close to Table Mountain near Cape Town, but they were soon eliminated as were others in areas to the north. By 1761 they no longer occurred south of the Oliphants River and by 1775 they had been eliminated in all the areas to the west of Port Elizabeth. In 1830 when elephant hunting within the Cape Colony was prohibited by the British Government, the hunters pressed northwards. The end result was the total removal of the elephant from most of South Africa, with the exception of parts of the north-western Transvaal, northern Zululand, the Knysna forests, and the Kruger and Addo National Parks.

The hunters now turned their attention to Central Africa. In 1897 Sir Harry Johnson described how elephants were becoming scarce in the 'Territory' (what is now Zambia) during the great hunting rush following David Livingstone's first expedition. Heavy hunting was also taking place in the Belgian Congo and throughout East Africa. Lt. Col. P. Offermann, who was a game and fish warden

Overleaf: **Plate 56.** When darkness falls, elephants continue their ceaseless eating and drinking. They have comparatively poor eyesight but a very keen sense of smell.

119

in the Congo, estimated that 585 000 elephants were killed there between 1889 and 1950.

When European farming methods were introduced to Central, East and West Africa the hunting of the elephant continued. We will never know exactly how many were killed, but conservative estimates put the figure at a minimum of one million between 1830 and 1930.

Within the last 50 years came the creation of national parks and wildlife reserves, with a simultaneous increase in control of elephant hunting. For a time, the decline of the elephant was halted. But as we have seen from earlier chapters there was also a redistribution of the remaining elephants, many of which concentrated inside the sanctuary boundaries, leading in turn to situations which made necessary culling programmes. This had the inevitable result of further reducing the total number of elephants in Africa.

The last decade has seen a new and tragic development in the story of the African elephant – the unprecedented growth of poaching, especially in East Africa. Jon Tinker reported in 1975 that an estimated 10 000 to 20 000 elephants were being killed each year *in Kenya alone*, and if this rate of poaching continued, the remaining elephants would be reduced to no more than a few hundred within a decade.

Nearly all the poaching was for ivory which eventually found its way overseas to end up as curios, piano keys and billiard balls; indeed there can be no doubt that the ivory trade is one of the main causes of the recent catastrophic decline of the African elephant. Tinker was told that in 1975 Kenya's ivory trade was worth a staggering ten million US dollars a year. However, very little of this revenue went to the Kenyan Government because in August 1974 the Minister of Tourism and Wildlife had banned all private dealings in ivory. It was a highly lucrative and illegal trade. World ivory prices had increased substantially in the ten years prior to 1975. Through the 1960's, it was stable at £1 per pound or six dollars per kilogram, but at the end of 1969 the price had risen to 30 dollars per kilogram. At those prices there was obviously a great deal of money to be made. In spite of the Government ban on ivory trading, on 5 March 1975 customs officials at Nairobi airport held up an ivory shipment due to be flown to Hong Kong where no doubt it would have been sold again or converted into curios to be sold at many times its original value. The shipment of 4 000 kilograms was worth at least 120 000 dollars. Who was behind it? Tinker's article presented evidence indicating that widespread corruption exists in Kenya, and that this corruption includes the illicit ivory trade.

As long as this most unsatisfactory state of affairs continues, the future for elephants in many parts of Kenya is bleak indeed. In a recent move, the Kenyan Government banned all forms of hunting and clamped down on the sale of curios. I am not altogether convinced this will help. Professional hunting, if controlled and supervised, as it certainly was in Kenya, is a perfectly legitimate form of conservation, and the number of animals killed each year was minute compared with the ravages of the poachers. Furthermore, the elephants and other species that were killed by the hunters brought in about £2,5 million a year in licence fees to the benefit of the whole country. It is also quite possible that the presence of the professional hunters and their clients in remote areas acted as a

122

deterrent as far as many of the poachers were concerned. In addition, a move towards a local and eventually world-wide ban in trade in elephant products might drive the trade underground which would make control even more difficult. It would also hit the legitimate ivory trade – for example the many tons obtained from control programmes in agricultural areas and culling programmes inside game reserves.

All the hunting and curio sale bans in the world will be totally ineffectual in the absence of efficient and dedicated law-enforcement officers who can rely on the full backing from the courts at all times, no matter how influential the culprit may be.

Of course, poaching is not restricted to Kenya – it is an unpalatable fact of life just about wherever elephants still occur. Uganda has an equally bad record. Recent counts by Keith Eltringham and Bob Malpas showed the following decline in elephant numbers:

Kabalega National Park	Rwenzori National Park
1973 ....14 309 elephants	1973 .... 2 731 elephants
1974 .... 6 030 elephants	1974 .... 1 907 elephants
1975 .... 2 246 elephants	1975 .... 1 047 elephants

These results showed that the Kabalega population had declined by 84,3%, and that at Rwenzori by 61,7%. More recent observations by Iain Douglas-Hamilton and Ian Parker indicate that the main cause was death rather than emigration, and an examination of Uganda's ivory export figures against recorded imports at Hong Kong show that there had been a great deal of illegal killing.

Poaching is a component of elephant mortality that is virtually impossible to measure, and yet its importance is so great that it makes a mockery of our attempts to predict elephant population trends in the years to come if our predictions are restricted to death by 'natural' causes.

At the start of this chapter I described the importance of mortality, especially mortality among the new-born, as a 'natural' population regulating mechanism. How do we measure this most important biological parameter and compare the mortality rates in different populations? The best method for illustrating the mortality schedule within any population of animals is by the construction of a 'survivorship curve' which starts with an initial cohort of 1 000 animals at birth and plots the number that survive through to the end of an animal's normal life-span – 60 years in the case of the African elephant (Fig. 19).

There are three methods which I will outline briefly, for collecting data for the construction of these curves. The first is where the age at death is directly observed from a large and reasonably random sample of the population. This is usually done from a collection of lower jaws found in the field, and this technique has been widely used throughout the world on a variety of species. The great disadvantage is that the carcasses of young animals tend to decay faster than those of adults. Furthermore, young animals are often completely eaten up by predators and scavengers, so that not a trace is left behind. I am quite sure that

Overleaf: **Plate 57.** A family unit of elephants at peace with the world, their trunks relaxed and temporal glands inactive.

123

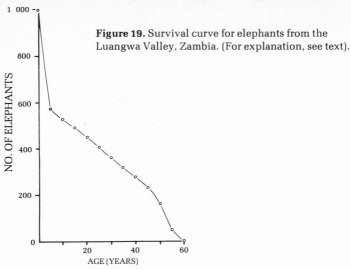

Figure 19. Survival curve for elephants from the Luangwa Valley, Zambia. (For explanation, see text).

hyaenas would make short work of a young elephant carcass. This inevitably results in an under-representation of young animals in a collection of found jaws.

Even most adult carcasses decay very rapidly; R. C. Morris found that two years was sufficient to remove *all* traces of dead adult Asiatic elephants, and the same could well apply to the African species in certain environments, although in the drier areas decomposition would take much longer. When I visited Addo Elephant Park near Port Elizabeth in South Africa at the end of 1977, Anthony Hall-Martin showed me some elephant limb bones that had been lying out in the open since 1920. After 57 years of exposure to weathering the bones were intact and easily recognisable.

In the second method of collecting information for survivorship curves, a large cohort born at more or less the same time is followed throughout its existence and a plot is made of all the animals that survive each year right through until the last animal dies. In the case of the elephant, this would be a 60 year study, which can hardly be considered a realistic proposition.

The third and final method is based on a shot sample. If the sample is random, the age structure for the population can be determined as I described in Chapter Four, and the number of animals dying in each age class can be inferred from the shrinking between successive age classes.

To obtain really worthwhile data on mortality there is no doubt that the second method, with more than one cohort under observation, is by far the best. Unfortunately, as this is all but totally unrealistic for an animal that lives for 60 years, most elephant studies based on post-mortem material have been forced to use the first or third methods, or a combination of the two. However, these two methods can be used *only* if the age structure of the population does not change with time, and as this is not always easy to determine, most of the published survivorship curves must be viewed with caution. The two methods can definitely *not* be used when certain age classes are stronger or weaker than they should be, as for example, immediately after a short period of very high mortality among the newborn. A survivorship curve constructed on the basis of information obtained from a sample shot just after a period when many young elephants have died would give a totally distorted estimate of the normal pattern of age-specific mortality.

In spite of all these difficulties, various attempts have been made to quantify the death rate in elephant populations, but it is often difficult to use this published information for comparative purposes because in many cases the methods used to estimate mortality were not always clearly defined, and the age-specific mortality rates were ambiguous, as the following four examples show.

One of the first references was provided by F. Bourlière and J. Verschuren in 1960 who stated that the mortality rate for the elephants in the Albert National Park in the Congo appeared to be very low (about 3%) and was probably twice as high for 'young animals' as for adults. In the following year I. O. Buss and A. C. Brooks described a '36% juvenile mortality' for elephants in Uganda. In the Kruger National Park in South Africa, U. de V. Pienaar postulated a mortality rate amongst 'very young calves' of as high as 33%. In 1968 Laws and Parker, describing the elephants on the North and South banks of the Murchison Falls Park in Uganda gave cumulative mortality rates up to 'two or three years of age' as 24% and 38% respectively.

It is, of course, impossible to equate references to mortality in 'young animals' or 'very young calves' with precise values that specify the actual ages involved, and under such circumstances I decided that comparisons are not really worthwhile.

However, the more recent studies, such as those of Dick Laws in 1969 and Timothy Corfield, which I mentioned earlier in this chapter, have provided much more precise data. For example, Laws produced estimates for elephant mortality in Tsavo based on a collection of found jaws, but he revised his mortality estimations by inserting additional deaths in the early age classes on the assumption that the younger animals were under-represented in his collection. He suggested that in Tsavo the average annual mortality for the female, aged six to 45 years, was 2% to 3%, as it appeared to be for the male aged six to 25 years. From birth to one year the mortality was 36%, and from one to five years it was 10%. After 45 years there was an increase in mortality in both sexes associated with tooth wear and a rapid decrease in the grinding area available for chewing food.

In contrast, Iain Douglas-Hamilton estimated that in the Lake Manyara area elephant mortality in the first year of life was only 10% and thereafter averaged between 3% to 4% annually.

It is quite clear that death rates in elephant populations vary not only throughout Africa but also within any one area or population as a result of local environmental extremes. Using all the published information I could find at the time, and my own data from Zambia, I prepared three hypothetical elephant survivorship curves, with low, medium and high mortality situations. I then used this information to investigate the importance of mortality in elephant population regulation in the population models I describe in Chapter Eight.

Overleaf: **Plate 58.** Another mock battle – the protagonists of the charade, two young bulls.

7
Elephant numbers, movement and social life

After two dry seasons in the Luangwa Valley, I was fairly optimistic that I would be able to use the vast amount of post-mortem material I had collected to produce some new and worthwhile information on the age-structure, growth and reproductive physiology of the local elephant population. What is more, I hoped that my study would make a contribution towards an understanding of the dynamics of the whole Luangwa ecosystem. On the other hand I appreciated that further comprehensive studies were required to complete the picture, not only on elephant feeding habits and their impact on the vegetation, but also on elephant numbers, their patterns of movement and, to a certain extent, their social life.

All these aspects were outside my terms of reference, but nevertheless some of these studies were taking place, unfortunately not all of them in the Luangwa.

To complete my story I must give a brief outline of the more important aspects of social life that are relevant to the elephant problem before describing some studies on elephant movement patterns and the estimation of their numbers.

Elephant society is essentially matriarchal; it is organised around a family unit of cows and their calves. The simplest group is a single adult female with one or more of her offspring but two or three such groups may be permanently associated. At puberty male elephants, usually driven out by the older females, leave the family units and join or form bachelor herds. Solitary females are very rare, and those that have been examined have all reached the end of their reproductive life, and the last molar, M_6, has been worn down to a fraction of its former size.

In his Lake Manyara study, Iain Douglas-Hamilton confirmed that the family unit was the basic stable social unit of elephant society. He also described a higher, slightly less stable association of two to four family units, numbering up to 50 animals, and suggested that this represented a 'kinship group'. Douglas-Hamilton's study of the social life of the elephant is undoubtedly the most outstanding contribution to this aspect of elephant biology, and his book *Among the Elephants* has made his work known to a wide public.

The association of family units and the bachelor herds into very big herds of several hundred is much more common in East Africa than in Central or southern Africa (Plate 59). It is generally accepted that these larger herds are formed

130

Plate 59. An aerial view of part of a very large herd of elephants.

following disturbance and disruption of the normal pattern of social life, in particular when the herd matriarch, or 'lead-cow' as she is often called, has been shot. Douglas-Hamilton has suggested that this bunching could have evolved largely from a need for collective defence against predators, including primitive man.

In contrast to the cows, the bull elephant groups are very temporary associations between similar animals who find themselves in the same place at the same time. Harvey Croze studied the bachelor elephants in Seronera where he recorded a short-term cohesion between bulls, with a greater tendency to group in the dry season. He recognised three main categories. First of all there were the

Overleaf: **Plate 60.** With the use of aeroplanes, elephant populations can be monitored throughout the year over the animals' total range. Estimates of the population can be fruitfully combined with studies of group size, herd composition and movement patterns.
Plate 61. Elephants often move in single file on their way to drink, and the well-worn elephant paths they follow are a characteristic feature of the African bush.

131

sexually non-competitive bulls, all of them capable of sperm production, but usually less than 25 years old. These males had not attained the requisite size and strength to compete with the older bulls for females. Next came the sexually competitive bulls, from 25 to 50 years old. These had attained full stature and could compete successfully for matings in a breeding herd. Finally, there were the 'retired' bulls, elephants that were probably more than 50 years of age. It is very likely that a similar social system exists with all bulls throughout other parts of the elephant's range.

In most applied behaviour studies, a biologist sets out to establish the way in which his animals are distributed in time and space. Do they have territories? How does the home range vary with season and group composition? To what extent can stress or disturbance influence the normal pattern of distribution and seasonal movements?

Dick Laws tried to answer some of these questions when he carried out an aerial survey of elephants in the Tsavo area of Kenya. He came up with the very interesting hypothesis that there were ten fairly *discrete* elephant populations in the whole ecological unit that extended over some 47 000 square kilometres. Each population was characterised by separate distributions and distinct population parameters, such as age structure, age at puberty and so on.

This idea stimulated a great deal of discussion as it was highly relevant to the management of elephants throughout their range. In other words, if Laws was right, killing elephants in one small part of Tsavo could well result in a considerable reduction in just one elephant population, whilst the other nine populations would not be affected at all.

Laws's hypothesis was based on aerial surveys, and because of its importance, further investigations were set up in an attempt to determine the boundaries of each distinct unit. Four years later Walter Leuthold and John Sale published the results of their studies. They had used radio-tracking techniques and observations on visually identifiable individuals, combined with two detailed aerial counts, to study elephant movements and patterns of habitat utilisation in the same Tsavo area. Their results showed that although a subdivision of the overall population into locally distinct units might have existed during the dry season, this was not the case after significant rainfall, when the elephants ranged over wide areas and came into contact with animals from other dry-season groups. Food appeared to be the primary factor governing movements and distribution of the elephants.

Leuthold and Sale's conclusions are difficult to reconcile with Laws's hypothesis and their work demonstrated the importance of combining various techniques to permit a sound interpretation of elephant movements. Nevertheless, these findings do not rule out the possibility that discrete sub-populations of elephants might exist elsewhere in Africa, and this should certainly be investigated.

There is no convincing evidence from anywhere in Africa of territorial behaviour in the elephant, although both bulls and family units do have a fairly distinct home range. There is a surprising lack of good data on the size of these home ranges, but what little information has been published indicates that an elephant's range varies tremendously in different habitat types. For example, in

Plate 62. This large termite mound has been broken open by elephants and black rhino, and much of the soil has been consumed.

the Lake Manyara area, Douglas-Hamilton found that the home ranges of family units and of individual bulls were widely overlapping and varied in size between 15 and 52 square kilometres. Leuthold and Sale recorded a mean home range of 350 square kilometres in Tsavo West, much less than the mean of 1 580 square kilometres in Tsavo East. These differences probably arise from the quality of the habitat as Tsavo East receives much less rainfall than both Tsavo West and Lake Manyara and therefore larger ranges are not unexpected.

Food quantity and quality, and the availability of water, are the most important factors determining when, where and how far elephants move. Comparatively small alluvial zones, such as those that occur in parts of the Zambezi Valley, can assume great significance for the elephant at the height of the dry season. Food, surface water and shade all remain readily available in these small areas in marked contrast to the drier, bare surrounding hills, and the elephants will modify their distribution accordingly.

There are other less obvious, but equally important factors influencing movement and distribution: one of these is the presence of sodium. It has been known for some time that elephants break open termite mounds and dig up and eat the soil (Plates 62 and 64), but nobody was quite sure why they did so. I saw elephants doing this several times in the Luangwa, and most of my observations were at the height of the rainy season. Not surprisingly, recent work by J. S. Weir

Overleaf: **Plate 63.** In the dry months of the year, adult elephants dig holes in dry, sandy river beds to search for subsurface water. When the herd moves off, other species, taking advantage of the holes the elephants have made, come down to drink.

Plate 64. From time to time elephants will dig up and eat soil that is rich in water-soluble sodium.

shows that the soil the elephants eat has high local concentrations of water-soluble sodium.

In most cases, the elephant's supply of sodium can be satisfied in the normal intake of water (Plates 21 and 55), but it is a significant observation that in Wankie National Park the highest density of elephants occurs at the waterholes with the highest sodium content. When sodium requirements cannot be met from the water, the elephants turn to the soil and, as might be anticipated, few elephants occur in regions with little sodium either in the water or in the soil.

From measurements of the mineral content of elephant dung, Weir concluded that the sodium content of the dung was too high to have come from plant food sources alone, indicating that saline water or soil are probably normal components of the elephant's diet.

We have made good progress in our attempts to get a clearer picture of some of the factors that influence the more detailed and localised elephant movement patterns, but there are still many blanks in our knowledge. Far from being just an interesting academic exercise, information on the 'why, when and where' of elephant movement is of vital concern to all biologists studying elephant problems; it is equally important to the wildlife manager who must implement elephant control programmes.

One of the best ways to study elephant movements is to record the resightings of marked animals, and the introduction of the powerful drug M.99 in the mid-1960s was a great boon to this type of research. A mere five milligrams of M.99 is sufficient to immobilise an adult bull elephant (Plate 72). Cows and calves require correspondingly smaller amounts. Within two or three minutes of receiving an intravenous injection of the antidote, M.285, the elephant is back on its feet again, none the worse for wear. As you may recall this was the drug we used in the Zambezi Valley capture operation.

The first elephant marking programmes in many parts of Africa – including the Luangwa – relied on the use of paints, collars and ear-tags (Plates 68, 69 and 70), but all of these had their disadvantages. For instance, an attempt to mark three elephants in Rhodesia with ear tags, ran into great problems: each tag consisted of two circular aluminium discs about 12 centimetres in diameter, one on each side of the ear. The two discs were connected by a polythene-covered steel bolt through a hole which was punched in the ear. Subsequently one of the elephants was seen with the disc missing and a large septic wound the same size as the disc in its place.

A young captive elephant was marked with one of these tags and kept under careful observation. The outer skin of the ear parted from the cartilage and over 200 millilitres of pus was collected from between the two layers.

Paint for marking purposes was also problematic. I tried marking elephants by painting them with the paint used for the white lines in the middle of tarred roads. Although it was useful for short-term identifications – and there was no doubt that the elephants were very conspicuous – after two or three weeks, the

Overleaf: **Plates 65, 66 & 67.** In the hot summer months, after drinking, elephants often plaster themselves with mud or blow dust all over their bodies to protect their skin from flies and from the burning rays of the sun.

paint was usually obscured by mud and dust and was often partially removed by the elephants rubbing themselves against trees. Even collars had their disadvantages: they were hidden behind the ears, were often surprisingly difficult to see, and any numbers or colours on them soon became obscured by mud.

More recently, biologists have been turning to the use of radio-transmitters, and some outstanding progress is being made in this field by Rowan Martin in Rhodesia. A collar with a radio-transmitter attached to the top of it is fitted around the immobilised elephant's neck (Plates 72 and 73). Soon after the antidote has been given the animal gets to its feet and moves off into the bush, the transmitter sending out signals that can be picked up at two or more fixed receivers each of which indicates the direction of the signal so that when two or more of these lines are plotted on a map it is possible to pinpoint the exact position of the animal. Hand-held receivers are used for relocation of the marked elephant in the field.

The advantages of radio-transmitters are obvious. Elephants can be tracked continuously over a period of months enabling us to build up a comprehensive picture of their movements. By being able to relocate these animals regularly, a biologist can record variations in group composition as each day goes by. Other marking devices do not have these advantages. It was not at all unusual for an elephant marked with paint and a collar to disappear completely for up to six months or more before the next resighting. By this time many of the marking devices were all but impossible to see.

White paint on the body is still useful for short-term studies where individual animals are followed immediately after the paint has been applied, as was demonstrated so successfully in Wyatt's and Eltringham's study of the daily activity of the elephants in the Rwenzori National Park in Uganda. I have already discussed their conclusions on feeding activity, but they also produced some useful observations on sleeping, drinking and home range. They reported that the elephant's typical pattern of rest was a prolonged sleep period in the small hours of the morning followed by a shorter rest period in the early afternoon. At night the sleep was deep, and most of the elephants lay down, their great bodies flattening the grass to form characteristic shaped elephant beds. The afternoon rest period was shorter, since the main purpose was not to sleep but to avoid the heat of the day.

None of the elephants lay down during the day, which could account for the fact that so few people have seen elephants lying down fast asleep.

Drinking occurred at any time of day or night (Plate 56), and was probably influenced more by the availability of water than by any other factor. On most days the elephants drank only once, while on other days they drank two or three times or even not at all.

On the whole, all the elephants studied had small home ranges, but there were records of elephants moving over considerable distances for short periods of time. Wyatt and Eltringham suggested that the elephants knew their home range in detail and that scent could be of great importance in orientation.

Plates 68-70. An immobilised elephant is painted as part of a marking programme. The antidote is given, and 'Z6' moves off into the mopane woodland.

The idea that elephants mark out and recognise a home range with scent is not a new one. For a long time naturalists have recorded broken bits of stick, bark and gravel embedded in the duct of the temporal gland on the side of the face, leading to the inevitable speculation that elephants rub their faces against trees and termite mounds to deposit temporal gland secretion and leave their scent behind.

While this might be so, I wanted further confirmation of temporal gland activity from both additional field observations and the post-mortem material from the abattoir. The latter did not give me any clues. There was quite clearly no obvious pattern connecting glandular activity with age, sex, season or reproductive status, and so I decided to observe the activity of the gland in the field at a time of the year when elephants were least disturbed by man. Naturally I selected the rainy season when few roads in the Luangwa South Reserve were open, and when the majority of the elephants rarely came in contact with vehicles or with man.

Furthermore I wanted to see how young elephants negotiated the mud and clinging, slippery clay and how they managed to cross over the swollen rivers. The shot sample from the abattoir had indicated to me that there was a fairly high death rate among the young, and I had speculated that accidents in the rains could be a significant contributing factor.

The two weeks I spent on these observations were the highlight of my time in Luangwa. All the rivers were in flood, and nearly all the roads in the South Game Reserve were closed. It was a joy to walk out of Mfuwe camp and know that I would not see another person for the whole day. Each day I found family units of elephants within a few kilometres of the camp, and I could not help but notice how they carefully avoided the particularly wet areas, especially when they had very young calves. Most of the time, the elephants were grazing on fresh lush *Echinochloa,* and with the exception of their occasional 'attacks' on big termite mounds which they would break open and eat for a few minutes, I saw nothing else of note.

After the hectic rush and trauma of the abattoir, it was an unbelievably pleasant change to watch elephants going about their day-to-day business undisturbed by man. Many of these animals had inactive temporal glands (Plate 57). I watched several of these groups for long periods, but if they were disturbed, it was quite common for me to see the temporal gland secretion begin a few seconds later, and in the more agitated individuals the secretion could be seen running down the side of the cheek.

I have subsequently observed an identical response among agitated elephants at much closer quarters in Addo Elephant Park. Elephants have comparatively poor sight, but a very keen sense of smell (Plate 53), and it is possible that the temporal gland is a means of communicating to other members of the family unit or herd that danger is at hand.

An interesting observation made by R. I. Pocock in 1916 seems to indicate that extinct relatives of the elephant also had a temporal gland. He described the palaeolithic engraving of a mammoth on a fragment of tusk found in a cavern,

Plate 71. Immersed in water, elephants refresh themselves.

Plate 72. A bull elephant has been immobilised with M.99, and a radio collar is being fitted to its neck.

Plate 73. With a radio collar firmly attached, and the antidote administered, the elephant makes its first attempt to get back to its feet.

and suggested that the streaks drawn on the side of the face represented a temporal gland larger and more active than in modern elephants.

As the wildlife areas of Africa shrink in size it is inevitable that sanctuaries will tend to become overcrowded, increasing the frequency of contact between the different herbivorous species. Territorial behaviour, when present, is an efficient method of spacing out animals *within* a species; but what happens when different species come together at the same waterhole? Will they tolerate one another? There appear to be very few known cases of aggression between different herbivores, and the elephant in particular seems remarkably tolerant of other animals and in turn is tolerated by them. An interesting exception was recorded by John Henshaw in the Yankari Game Reserve in Nigeria where he witnessed what was probably a territorial male waterbuck defending his area from the advances of a small herd of elephants. As the elephants approached, the waterbuck ceased feeding, watched the elephants for a few minutes, and then walked towards them. A large elephant trumpeted, walked slowly towards the waterbuck, shook its head several times, and then charged. The waterbuck ran off, but circled back to within 60 metres of two elephants standing slightly apart from the main group, bobbing his head and presenting his horn tips towards them. He then ran directly towards the elephants, causing them 'to flee with raised tails and outstretched trunks into the main herd'. Aggression between two species has been termed *taxogenic aggression*, and it can be regarded as an overspill from the normal pattern of territorial behaviour seen between animals of the same species, perhaps a consequence of overcrowding in the artificial confines of a wildlife reserve.

In the years to come it will be of immense value to wildlife managers to be familiar with all aspects of behaviour of the animals in their regions. Elephants moving in flight and 'standing-tall' when alarmed can be recognised quite easily (Plates 74 and 75), as can sex play between young bulls and a range of other equally characteristic postures (Plates 13, 58 and 71).

The recognition of *taxogenic aggression* might not be so easy, and yet this could be a most useful indication of behavioural stress factors, and would thus be of significance in management.

A great deal of time, effort and money has been spent on estimating elephant numbers throughout the continent, and this was intensified in 1976 with the launching of the combined International Union for the Conservation of Nature and World Wildlife Fund (IUCN/WWF) Elephant Survey and Conservation Programme. Before I describe this survey, I would like to go back to some of the earlier attempts to estimate elephant numbers to illustrate how most of the populations were initially seriously under-estimated.

The apparent spectacular growth of the elephant population in the Luangwa Valley is an excellent case in point. In 1897 Mr H. Johnston visited what was then British Central Africa and noted that 'elephants remain abundant in the Mweru Marsh and the Luangwa Valley'. Seven years later, Sir Alfred Sharpe produced one of the first attempts at a 'game census':

'The Society of Arts have been favoured with permission from the Secretary of State for Foreign Affairs, to publish the following game census – which is covered by the letter to Sir Clement Hill, K.C.M.G., C.B., Superintendent of African Protectorates – from Sir Alfred Sharpe, K.C.M.G., C.B.

Dear Sir Clement,
Before I left British Central Africa for England on leave last year, I requested all the collectors of the Protectorate to fill in forms for the obtaining of something in the way of a 'Game Census'. This has been done, and I now forward it to you. While, of course, many of the items entered are extremely uncertain, the general proportions in which game of different descriptions is present in various districts are fairly reliable. I should put the number of elephants at more like 1 500 than 600.

Yours sincerely,
Alfred Sharpe.

The Residency, Zomba,
British Central Africa.
January 25, 1904.'

In 1934 Captain Charles Pitman gave a figure of 7 000 elephants in the 'Upper and Middle Luangwa Valley'. The next estimate was made in 1951 by W. E. Poles, who gave figures for each of the different reserves within the valley. His estimate for the South Reserve was 929 elephants. When Johnny Uys carried out the first aerial survey in the Luangwa in 1964 his estimate for the South Reserve was 15 000 elephants. Nine years later an aerial survey by Graeme Caughley and John Goddard produced an estimate of 31 600 elephants for the same area!

We will never know how much of this increase was due to a compression of the elephant's range combined with the natural increase of the population, but from our knowledge of the general distribution of elephants in the Luangwa and from the fact that it is most unlikely that an elephant population would grow at more than 4% per year, most of the increase must be attributed to an improvement in counting techniques. Caughley went on to suggest that the estimates for the whole Luangwa drainage area would almost certainly top 100 000 if unsurveyed areas within the valley were included, and this far and away exceeds reported estimates of numbers from other areas of continuous range in Africa.

The detailed aerial surveys carried out by Graeme Caughley and his colleagues in various months complemented the other studies of elephant movements. Within the South Game Reserve they found that elephants moved towards the alluvial zone about one month after the rains began. By January the process was completed, and the alluvium held densities averaging seven elephants per

Plate 74. An elephant 'stands tall' after being disturbed by an intruder while drinking at Lake Kariba.

square kilometre, whereas in the remainder of the reserve the density had dropped to two per square kilometre. The elephants started to move away from the rivers by March, and by May they had taken up their dry season pattern of distribution with an even density throughout the reserve.

Earlier on in this book (Chapter Six, p 106) I called attention to the fact that the African elephant is being seriously threatened in many parts of the continent, not only by poaching but also by the destruction of its natural habitat associated with modern agriculture. We know this is happening, but we still have very little reliable information on the status of elephant in most parts of the continent, and we do not know how the authorities in individual countries view the economic value of the elephant.

An initiative to answer these and other questions came from the New York Zoological Society, and subsequently the International Union for the Conservation of Nature (IUCN) and its close associate World Wildlife Fund International, who combined to launch the 'Elephant Survey and Conservation Programme'. According to the project description, the basic objective is 'to assess the current status and future prospects of the African and Asian elephants, and to recommend an action programme to IUCN/WWF for improving the conservation of these species. The ultimate goal will be to encourage people and governments to value elephants both for their intrinsic value and for their economic potential as a 'self-sustaining natural resource'.

Iain Douglas-Hamilton and Harvey Croze are co-chairmen of the African elephant specialist group, and they have already begun their programme with the distribution of a questionnaire to official and private sources. From this, and their own field research, they plan to delineate current elephant ranges, produce initial population estimates, and determine the main trends in elephant population dynamics.

By the end of 1977 the programme had published two newsletters. In the first, Douglas-Hamilton reported on an aerial survey he had completed in the 55 000 square kilometre Selous Game Reserve in Tanzania. He estimated that the reserve contained a minimum of 81 600 elephants. For once, the elephants did not appear to be causing significant damage to the woody vegetation, and there was no evidence to suggest that their range was being compressed. In fact, the opposite appeared to be true, as they had invaded areas formerly occupied by man.

The programme's second newsletter contained a provisional map of known elephant distribution up to January 1977, with the comment: 'The continental picture is still very far from complete, and in most cases we cannot yet hazard a guess at elephant numbers within a country.'

The IUCN/WWF survey has a big task ahead. It is impossible for members of the Elephant Specialist Group to undertake surveys such as the one carried out in the Selous Game Reserve for the whole continent, and they will have to rely on the co-operation of the wildlife authorities in the relevant countries if the programme is to achieve what it set out to do.

It is beyond the scope of this book to give details of the various aerial counting techniques and the problems associated with their use. Suffice it to say that aerial surveys of elephant populations have undoubtedly opened up new

150

dimensions for both the research worker and the wildlife manager. Many of the population estimates of the past were based on very limited census techniques and more often than not the survey was carried out on foot in a small part of the total range at a limited time of the year. With the use of aeroplanes has come year-round population monitoring over the animals' total range, and estimates of populations have often been combined with studies of group size, herd composition and patterns of movement (Plate 60).

Improved counting techniques, coupled with a better understanding of the relevant aspects of elephant behaviour, must lead eventually to better management of the species, and so help to ensure its survival.

8
The future
for elephants
in Africa

Carol, Jonathon and I left Zambia at the end of 1970 and returned to Cambridge where I faced the task of some final data analysis and the writing of my thesis. University life was a welcome and stimulating contrast to the academic isolation of the Luangwa Valley, and I was quick to appreciate the advantages of discussing the relevance and significance of my own study with people from a range of different disciplines. Cambridge gave me a chance to sit down and think about what I had been doing in Zambia, and to ask some searching questions on the future for elephants throughout their range.

In the first few weeks I turned my attention to the theories of population growth and regulation as this was fundamental to the elephant problem. I had come to appreciate that in the evolution of African ecosystems, complex and dynamic changes had occurred that involved the composition, distribution and status of most of the species of animals and plants.

With long-term climatic changes, living organisms interacted with one another and their environment so that only the fittest survived. When water-tables fell and plant communities changed, the herbivores and, in their turn the carnivores, changed as well. In short, nature thrived on dynamic interactions, but at the same time always sought stability, so that animal populations tended to stabilise or fluctuate at a level in balance with their environmental resources. If this stability had not existed, populations would have experienced wild fluctuations and oscillations, but we believe that in most cases this did not occur in a natural African ecosystem.

In relatively undisturbed parts of Africa, populations are still regulated by a combination of three factors: variations in the birth-rate, death rate and migration; a concept that can be summarised in a simple curve (Fig. 20). At low population densities, when there is no shortage of food, water and space, the population growth rate will be high. The birth-rate will be high, the death rate low, and animals may immigrate. As the numbers increase, food and space are less readily available. The birth-rate declines, the death rate increases, and the surplus animals emigrate. With relatively stable climatic conditions in an undisturbed ecosystem, a situation can be reached where animals are in harmony with one another and with their food supply.

152

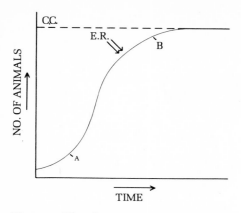

Figure 20. The relationship between growth in population and the carrying capacity (C.C.). At low population density (A), the birth-rate is high, the death rate low, and animals may immigrate. The general growth rate is high. At high population density (B), environmental resistance (E.R.) slows down the rate of population growth. The birth-rate declines, the death rate increases, and the surplus animals emigrate.

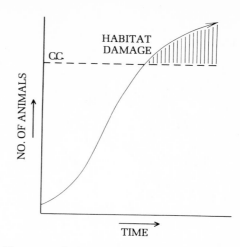

Figure 21. The basis of the elephant problem — emigration no longer possible and immigration too rapid for the normal population regulatory mechanism to cope, the carrying capacity is exceeded, and damage to the habitat follows.

This is, of course, an over-simplification, as there will always be climatic irregularities with a concomitant change in the vegetation, which in turn will result in both short and long-term fluctuations in the animal populations. Nevertheless, the population growth curve shown in Fig. 20 does serve as a useful basis for discussion, and is widely used as such in studies of animal populations.

I believe that elephant populations also follow this growth form, but recently something has gone wrong. The increasing human population has taken over much of the elephants' range so that emigration can no longer be considered as a population regulating mechanism – the elephants have nowhere left to move to. In fact, at a time when the surplus animals should be emigrating, most elephant populations are experiencing rapid *immigration* (Fig. 21). And as more elephants move in, we can anticipate that the birth-rate will continue to fall and the death rate increase until the population declines once more to a level in keeping with the food supply. If our hypothesis is right, then is it necessary to introduce elephant culling programmes? Can't we leave it to nature?

To help me answer these questions, one of my first priorities was to find out to what extent variations in the birth rate (reproductive homeostasis) and variations in mortality actually regulate an elephant population. The calculations involved in a study of this kind can be so involved, time-consuming and laborious that without the aid of a computer several weeks' work would be necessary to produce any worthwhile results. I decided to construct some mathematical 'models' of elephant populations using the Titan Computer of the University of

153

Cambridge Computing Service, and I soon became totally absorbed in what I found to be a very exciting line of research.

Together with Jim McIntosh from the Agricultural Research Council in Cambridge, we constructed population models based on realistic parameters from comparative studies of elephant populations in East Africa and Zambia. We had to 'feed in' variations in mortality, age at puberty, age at which reproduction ceased, and mean calving interval, and I decided to use the following variables:

Variations in mortality (Figures shown are for % mortality/year).

Age	Low mortality	Medium mortality	High mortality
1st four years	5	10	20
5-45 years	1	1,5	4
46-55 years	4	5	50
56-60 years	50	50	—

Variations in age at puberty

12 years
17 years
22 years

Variations in age at reproductive senescence

45 years
50 years
55 years

Variations in mean calving interval

3 years   7 years
4 years   8 years
5 years   9 years
6 years

For each of the three mortality rates, we programmed the computer to calculate a total of 63 values for the rate of population increase in groups of nine as shown below:

Low mortality elephant population

Mean three year calving interval

Puberty at 12 years	Rate of increase
Breeding ends at 45 years	4,68%
Breeding ends at 50 years	4,72%
Breeding ends at 55 years	4,73%

Puberty at 17 years

Breeding ends at 45 years	3,65%
Breeding ends at 50 years	3,80%
Breeding ends at 55 years	3,86%

Puberty at 22 years

Breeding ends at 45 years	2,69%
Breeding ends at 50 years	2,96%
Breeding ends at 55 years	3,11%

In the subsequent eight groups of calculations based on the low mortality situation, the mean calving interval was progressively increased by one year in each case. The calculations were then repeated in turn for the other two mortality schedules to give a total of 189 values for the rate of population increase.

The results of this study were most revealing and rewarding. Of the three reproductive homeostatic mechanisms we considered, changes in the calving interval had the greatest influence on the rate of population increase. But the most important conclusion was that although all these variations in reproduction can and do influence the rate of population increase, the most important single population controlling mechanism is variation in the death rate, especially among the new-born.

In terms of the elephant problem this is a very important conclusion, because it means that even if the elephant populations were to bring about substantial reductions in their birth-rates, in the absence of a significant increase in mortality, the corresponding reduction in growth rates would never be adequate to compensate for the increased immigration. In other words, without further increases in the death rate, the elephant problem cannot be solved by the elephants themselves unless we are prepared to accept the 'solution' of unparalleled habitat destruction and a massive die-off of thousands of elephants.

More recently several other studies have called attention to the importance of *survival of the young* in regulating populations of long-lived mammals. Lee Eberhardt in particular has stressed that security of the adult population is the key to the persistence of such species, and the *last* parameter to give way to the pressures of over-population may thus be adult female survival.

One other interesting fact to emerge from these models was that under ideal ecological conditions, with overall low mortality, a mean three year calving interval, puberty at 12 years and breeding continuing until 55 years, an elephant population increases at 4,73% or 47 elephants per thousand elephant per year. As it is unlikely that an elephant population would be able to maintain such a high reproductive performance, we concluded that an annual population increase of 4% is probably close to the maximum.

A significant and noteworthy exception to this 4% rate of increase was given to me recently by Anthony Hall-Martin in the Addo Elephant Park. In 1953 the Park contained 17 elephants; these increased to 94 by 1978, representing a 7% rate of increase. A possible explanation for this very high rate of increase could be a high rate of reproduction coupled with a low neonatal and juvenile death rate in the comparatively secure and protected sanctuary of the Park, especially as the elephants were, until very recently, given regular supplementary food.

Malthus, who wrote in 1798, may guide us in the operation of population self-regulatory mechanisms. He believed that two factors control human population, 'misery' and 'vice'. By 'misery' he meant disease, starvation and homelessness, and 'vice' included war and social conflict. Turning to elephants, for the word 'misery' let us substitute nutritional deficiencies, and for 'vice' let us substitute social pressure. We assume that in the elephant world the birth-rate falls as elephant population density reaches certain critical levels, but we have still to establish whether this reduction is caused by either or both a decline in nutritional status or an increase in social pressures.

The Lake Manyara elephant study gives us a clue as to the main controlling factor. Manyara has one of the highest known elephant densities in Africa, with about five elephants per square kilometre. Yet in spite of this high density, the mean age at puberty is about 11 years and the mean calving interval about four and a half years. This strongly suggests that high density per se is not necessarily a regulatory mechanism, and that the food supply is much more important. If nothing else, this example shows that comparisons of density measurements alone are meaningless without reference to vegetation type, condition and trend, and also the degree of social interaction within the elephant population.

I should point out that not all biologists accept the 'compression hypothesis' as the basis of the elephant problem. Writing in the final FAO Luangwa Valley report, and later in the East African Wildlife Journal, Graeme Caughley reviewed existing hypotheses on the elephant problem and came to the conclusion that there is no attainable natural equilibrium between elephants and forests. He visualised the natural condition as a cyclical relationship in which elephants increase while thinning out the forests and then decline again when trees become too sparse. According to his view, when the elephants reach low numbers the forests are free once more to regenerate, and with increasing tree cover the elephants in turn begin to increase once more.

Caughley therefore suggests that the salient characteristics of the cyclic relationship are trends in which elephants and trees are similar to sine waves, that of trees being about one quarter of a wavelength behind that of elephants. This is known as a stable limit cycle, and Caughley proposed that with the elephants the cycle period from peak to peak (or trough to trough) is between 150 and 240 years. The cycle hypothesis implies that the 'elephant problem' is characteristic of the system, and consequently in the Luangwa Valley the elephant density must presently be close to a peak. Over the next ten years or so the population can be expected to commence a slow decline, with the density of trees continuing to decline over the same period. This will continue until the elephants reach a density between half or two thirds of that at present, and at that point the rate at which the trees are thinned out will slow down and the trend will be reversed. Caughley had two main lines of evidence for this suggestion: the first was based on the pattern of the age structure and damage of mopane and baobab trees which indicated possible long-term cycles of utilisation; the second was negative in that other hypotheses were unsatisfactory for the Luangwa Valley.

Caughley's attractive and elegant hypothesis has certainly introduced a new dimension to the elephant problem, and it deserves further consideration. If nothing else, he has highlighted the need for more detailed comparative long-term studies of elephant population dynamics and of elephant/habitat inter-relationships in different parts of the continent.

Unfortunately, historical and current evidence from other parts of Africa cast doubt on his stable limit cycle hypothesis. The reasons are as follows.

An essential part of Caughley's argument is the relationship between trees and elephants. 'Elephants increase while thinning out the forest and then decline again when trees become too sparse. When elephants decline to low numbers the trees are able once more to regenerate, and with increasing tree cover the elephants again begin to increase,' he says.

This implies that elephants must have trees to survive. When tree density is reduced, then a decline in the elephant population will follow. Caughley does not attempt to elucidate the *proximate factors* involved in this population decline. Presumably he envisages an increase in the death rate coupled with a reduction in the rate of reproduction.

I know of no evidence anywhere in Africa to support this *direct* tree/elephant relationship, but quite clearly it calls for further, more detailed studies.

In the Luangwa Valley 95% of the elephants' diet during the rains is fresh green grass with its high protein content, and it appears that this is the essential proximate factor that stimulates ovulation and fertile mating. Elephants change to browse in the dry season, and obviously an adequate supply of browse is required during these critical months. A decline in the rate of reproduction and an increase in mortality will almost certainly follow a sustained reduction in the plane of nutrition, but would a 50% reduction in tree density have a significant effect on the plane of nutrition and in turn on elephant population dynamics?

Caughley's illustration of two sine waves, 'that of trees being about one quarter of a wavelength behind that of elephants' implies that it would, and that this reduction in population growth rate would have come about gradually over a number of years. It is important to remember that by its very nature, a stable limit cycle is in *marked contrast* to the massive and sudden die-off in Tsavo that I described in Chapter Six (p.106), and consequently we would anticipate that near the peaks of elephant population density in Caughley's cycle, at a point where tree density has been declining for a number of years, there should be some initial evidence of either increased mortality or decreased fecundity. This is certainly not borne out by the elephants I examined in the Luangwa Valley nor those I looked at more recently in Rhodesia – both areas where tree density has declined significantly in recent years.

The elephants in the Budongo Forest in Uganda, with its superabundance of trees – and one of the latest mean ages at puberty recorded (22,8 years) – do not support Caughley's hypothesis either.

Finally, and perhaps most important of all, if the cycle period from peak to peak is about 200 years, then about 100 years ago the Luangwa Valley and many parts of Rhodesia and East Africa should have had a low density of elephants, and a severely damaged or degraded forest in the early stages of recovery. I know of no historical evidence from any journal of that time to support this idea.

I bring up these arguments not because I want to enter into an academic debate, but *because I am deeply concerned by the general lack of appreciation and awareness of the immediate consequences of the very high rates of human population growth on the future of the wildlife populations of Africa.* There is already an overwhelming body of evidence to show that compression has brought about the elephant problem throughout the animals' range.

The Chizarira elephant problem I described in detail in Chapter Two (p.19) is a classic case that supports the compression hypothesis, and more recently Laws, Parker and Johnstone in their book *Elephants and their Habitats* have given an excellent account of the way in which the expanding human population has displaced elephants from most of their former range in the Bunyoro District of Uganda.

There is every indication that there are going to be further considerable reductions in the elephants' range in Africa in the years to come. Four words sum up the threat to wildlife and its habitat: exponential human population growth. It is a threat that exists in all the African countries that I mention in this book (Table 3 and Fig. 22).

Table 3. Total human population, growth rates and doubling time for seven African countries referred to in the text.

Country	1974 Population Estimate	Growth rate	Doubling Time (yrs)
Botswana	670 000	3,1%	22,4
Kenya	12 900 000	3,3%	21,0
Rhodesia	6 100 000	3,6%	19,3
South Africa	24 300 000	2,9%	23,9
Tanzania	14 800 000	2,5%	27,7
Uganda	11 200 000	3,0%	23,1
Zaire	24 200 000	2,1%	33,0

We cannot afford to be indifferent to these statistics in the vague hope that the birth-rates will soon decline. It is essential to understand that human population growth has a powerful momentum that persists for years and years. There are

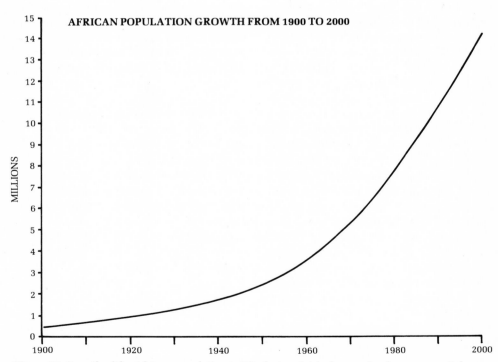

Figure 22. Growth of the African population in Rhodesia, a typical example of an exponential growth curve. At the turn of the century, there were 500 000 people – at the end of this century there will be an estimated 14 100 000.

two reasons for this. Firstly, the high birth-rate that causes the population explosion cannot be changed overnight. The developed countries required several generations to bring about substantial fertility reduction, and the same must still apply today in the developing regions of Africa. The second and less evident basis for the momentum of population growth is the large proportion of children found in the populations of the developing countries. In all of the countries in Table 3, 45% of the population is under 15 years of age. In a generation most of these individuals will become parents themselves, and will inevitably produce their own big families. Even if all future couples were to have only enough children to replace themselves, the population would still increase substantially before levelling off.

I must point out that the figures given in Table 3 can be deceptive because human populations should not be considered in isolation as a simple total of the number of people living in a country. The impact these people make on their environment and the threat they pose to wildlife, is determined by the way they are distributed in relation to the *quantity* and *quality* of the land available for their use.

Two examples, one from Rhodesia, and the other from Natal in South Africa, well illustrate these points. Under the system of land tenure operating in Rhodesia in 1974, 180 190 square kilometres were designated Tribal Trust Lands for the black population. In that year just over 60% of the black population occupied these lands, and much of this land *surrounded* the major wildlife sanctuaries. If present population trends continue, it is anticipated that the number of people in the Tribal Trust Lands will double in the next 19 years. The undesirability of such an increase under present systems of land use is demonstrated by the following quotation from Rhodesia's Natural Resources Board Annual Report for 1973.

For many years now, the Board has emphasised the serious and deteriorating ecological situation prevailing in the Tribal Trust Lands. The problem may now well be reaching a magnitude which will be incapable of solution, and which could destroy the economic stability of the country.
Uncontrolled expansion of human and animal populations combined with primitive and destructive methods of husbandry have placed an intolerable burden on the soil, water and vegetation resources of nearly half the land surface of Rhodesia. In an underpopulated situation, resource misuse is criminal. In an overpopulated situation, it is suicidal. In many of the Tribal Trust Lands, particularly in the south of the country, natural resources have already been degraded. In certain areas destruction has reached near disaster levels, where even a subsistence economy can be sustained only with difficulty.

For a respected organisation which does not resort to extravagant language, such a report speaks for itself. It is worth noting that as long ago as 1960, V. Vincent and R. G. Thomas drew attention to the poor agricultural potential of Tribal Trust land in Rhodesia (Fig. 23).

Nine years later, Professor George Kay showed that 57% of the designated

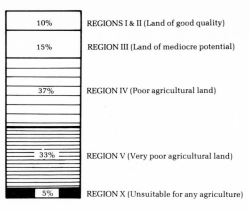

10%	REGIONS I & II (Land of good quality)
15%	REGION III (Land of mediocre potential)
37%	REGION IV (Poor agricultural land)
33%	REGION V (Very poor agricultural land)
5%	REGION X (Unsuitable for any agriculture)

Figure 23. African land in Rhodesia, classified after Vincent and Thomas (1960).

Tribal Trust areas were overpopulated and grossly overpopulated. In spite of this, these overpopulated areas continued to support high densities of people, but while doing so the inevitable downward spiral of deterioration was intensified. Of course, under such conditions, many wildlife species have been eliminated or driven out. Elephants in particular had no place in the white-owned farming lands, and with the added pressures from the Tribal Trust Lands, their only sanctuaries were the wildlife reserves. A few elephants remain in some of the Tribal Trust Lands, but these animals will be subjected to inevitable harassment until they, too, disappear.

In Natal, in South Africa, parts of KwaZulu provide a further frightening example of the end result of a rapidly growing population that practises primitive agriculture in a limited area of land. In 1973 the population of KwaZulu was 2 320 995, and the growth rate was 3,5% per year, which meant that the population would double every 19,8 years. The story is essentially the same as Rhodesia, with the added complication that only 23% of the land can be classified as flat or undulating and generally suitable for growing crops – the remainder is hilly or mountainous. Over two thirds of KwaZulu can be regarded as land of poor quality, unsuited to cultivation. In 1975 Natal lost an estimated 200 million tons of soil by erosion into the sea, and there can be no doubt that much of this was a consequence of too many people and domestic stock in too small an area, with the added disadvantage of continued primitive forms of land use in hilly country with fragile soils. Indigenous woodland is disappearing rapidly from parts of KwaZulu and in the eyes of many of the local people, wildlife has no part to play. Furthermore there is no hope of their becoming more sympathetic to the cause of conservation when their own numbers have doubled in 20 years' time.

Early in 1975 the UN/FAO warned that chronic overgrazing in 37 Middle Eastern and African countries was turning 21 million square kilometres of fertile land into desert. Yet in spite of this, so many African countries go on doing what history has clearly shown to be wrong; the extension of cultivation into the hilly districts and poorer soils of Africa.

160

An extreme example is the overgrazing and deforestation of the Sahel which has led to the Sahara encroaching by up to 50 kilometres a year on a broad front. In the Sahel thousands of people starved to death; we have every reason to believe that with present high rates of population growth and primitive forms of land use, it is inevitable that this pattern will be repeated in other parts of Africa in the very near future.

Against such a background, with poverty, hunger, lack of educational and health facilities, and land shortages facing so many parts of the continent, can we expect the poorer countries of Africa to devote a large share of their budget to the 'preservation' of national parks and wildlife reserves?

To help resolve this dilemma, we can profit by looking at the report on a mission accomplished for UNESCO in 1960 by the late Sir Julian Huxley. Describing the conservation of wildlife and natural habitats in Central and East Africa he wrote: 'Let me state the African situation in ecological terms. The ecological problem is fundamentally one of balancing resources against human needs, both in the short and in the long term. It must thus be related to a proper evaluation of human needs, and it must be based on resource conservation and resource use, including optimum land use and conservation of the habitat.' Huxley was calling attention to the necessity for evaluating human needs, and then meeting these requirements by planning the *long-term conservation of all available resources,* a philosophy far removed from present-day African practices.

It follows that if all the wildlife species and their habitats are to survive in Africa — and hold their own against the demands of man — they must all become part of a multi-disciplinary form of land use and be subjected to 'wise-use' as and when necessary. In other words we must justify our desire to conserve wildlife, and make sure that our terms are compatible with the very demanding needs of developing countries.

Aesthetic and cultural factors are important, but it is my conviction that the economic and ecological considerations alone will determine the survival of many of the wildlife areas. Food and economics have high priority, so that if wildlife populations can produce worthwhile quantities of protein and earn foreign exchange on a sustained yield basis, an economic justification for conservation is likely to gain wide support.

Gradually, the economic value of wildlife resources is gaining acceptance in African countries, and this could be the most important single contributing factor guaranteeing the promotion and implementation of realistic conservation policies. Tourism, meat production, the sale of skins, ivory and even the sale of live animals for restocking other areas or for zoos, all generate revenue. Furthermore, hundreds of local people are employed in associated industries which promise immense potential for further expansion. A simple example is the development of African skills to produce high-quality hand-made leather goods for the overseas market.

In Kenya, tourism in 1972 was the principal foreign exchange earner, grossing over 75 million US dollars, and elephants play their part in attracting the visitor to Africa as much as, if not more than, any other species.

It seems without dispute that cropping of animals on a sustained yield basis is an entirely complementary form of land use which need not conflict with tourism. There will always be a big demand for meat from the urban centres, and the ready availability of cheap meat to local markets could well act as an incentive to reduce poaching.

Even Botswana, with its comparatively small human population, gains very worthwhile revenue from its wildlife resources. In 1973 the total value of wildlife in the Botswana economy was just under ten million US dollars, and this included tourism and all forms of hunting by both resident and visiting hunters.

Hard statistics might make good sense, but they will not have universal appeal. Daphne Sheldrick summed up the opposite point of view when she was discussing the Tsavo elephant problem. She wrote: 'It is difficult to make certain people understand that there is a widespread public revulsion against the concept that the surviving stocks of wildlife must be treated as a "consumable natural resource". We have consumed too much of the world's resources already: in fact, more in the last 25 years than during the rest of man's occupation of this planet.' I can understand this point of view, but faced with all the problems associated with the realities of human exponential population growth, have we any alternative but to promote a 'wise-use' conservation policy in contrast to the inflexible 'preservationists'?

While the economic value of wildlife is now widely accepted in Africa, certainly among the developing nations, I believe that the *ecological* value of wildlife is probably even more important as a justification for conservation. But as the benefits are very often indirect, and as they have no immediate economic value, they receive little publicity and are poorly understood.

What, then, is the ecological value of wildlife species? By wildlife, I am referring to every single living organism in the plant and animal kingdoms with the exception of the domesticated species, and this includes the many thousands of species that live outside the boundaries of wildlife sanctuaries. The value of these organisms stems from their essential and active participation in immense and complex ecological systems, such as the water, carbon, oxygen and nitrogen cycles. It is often not acknowledged that man, and his domestic plants and animals, are utterly dependent for their existence on the efficient functioning of these complex cycles. For example, we depend on them for such vital functions as the preservation of the atmosphere, the disposal of our waste material, and the recycling of the nutrients that are used by our food plants. Soils themselves (one of the many things we take for granted and are so guilty of mismanaging) are the product of the interaction of a great variety of living organisms with inorganic and organic particles.

Equally important is the rôle of wildlife species in maintaining ecological stability. Erosion and floods are reduced in areas with well-developed natural plant communities, and there is no doubt that the elimination of these communities has given rise to serious loss of soil in far too many parts of Africa; there is every indication that this trend is accelerating.

All too often we tend to overlook the essential inter-relationships that exist in wildlife ecosystems. I quote as an example the important rôle the impala plays in seed germination in several areas of Africa. The seed pods of *Acacia tortilis* are greatly favoured by impala, and when the seeds pass through the animals'

162

digestive system, the gastric juices soften the seeds and encourage rapid and successful germination. Experiments have shown that dry seed pods fail to germinate.

The impala, then, is a vital link in maintaining a healthy tree population. Like animals, trees die of old age. On the ground, the termites take over and break them down very quickly, carrying vast quantities of dead material below the surface, eventually creating small islands of rich soil. In the process of constructing their mounds, damp soil is carried up again, providing a favourable site for the germination of seeds. In places, the bigger termite mounds provide an ideal site for the growth of the sweeter and more palatable species of grass, which in turn the impala graze upon in the drier months of the year. We have thus gone full-circle back to the impala.

But this is just part of the story, for many other animals come into this cycle. Termite mounds are a study in themselves. In addition to providing a habitat for grasses, trees which do not grow in the surrounding areas, grow there. Some of the larger African predators, such as the lion and cheetah, use them as lookout points from which to select a suitable victim. Other species still use smaller termite mounds as central vantage points in their territories. Elephants use them as scratching posts, and elephants and rhino break open some of the bigger mounds and eat the salt that has been concentrated in the soil.

Then come the species that feed on the termites themselves, three fascinating and unrelated mammals, the aardvark, the aardwolf and the pangolin. The impala itself is preyed upon by leopard, lion, cheetah and wild dog, and the acacia tree provides browse for the giraffe and nesting sites for the weavers. At a first casual glance, it would be difficult to imagine that such inter-relationships could exist.

Elephants also play their part in this complex of interactions. Like the impala, they are vital in the rôle of seed dispersers. Indeed, in the Luangwa Valley it is common to see *Acacia albida* seedlings growing out of elephant dung. The dung consists of a great deal of fibrous vegetable material which forms an ideal germination medium for seeds that escape crushing by mastication and then pass undigested through the elephant's alimentary canal. In fact, there is evidence that this passage greatly facilitates germination. Elephants distribute nutrients in their dung as well, which are in turn carried below ground by termites and dung beetles.

Another positive rôle played by elephants is that at times they provide water for other species, for instance, making subsurface supplies available to others by digging holes in the sand (Plate 63). They also paddle in shallow depressions, their immense weight compressing the soil and trapping the rainfall. Subsequently they may plaster large amounts of mud on their bodies which is carried away, making the waterholes even deeper (Plates 65, 66 and 67). Elephant paths often lead to waterholes, and these well-worn tracks can stop the spread of destructive bush-fires (Plate 61). In short, elephants do not exist in isolation. They interact with many other species of plants and animals, and their presence in an African ecosystem helps to maintain diversity, adding to their ecological value.

In this book, I set out to explain how the elephant problem came into being, and I have concluded that man's inability or unwillingness to control his own numbers precipitated the problem. I have also concluded that the elephant problem cannot be solved by the elephants themselves, unless we are prepared to accept the solution of unparalleled habitat destruction and a massive die-off of thousands of these great animals. Intervention by man, namely elephant culling and fire control, provides the only realistic alternative, and this, in essence, was the main recommendation to come from the final report of the Luangwa Valley Conservation and Development Project.

However, as each day goes by, compression of the elephants' range continues, and with exponential human population growth an established fact of life, the elephant problem seems here to stay. In fact, the very existence of elephants is now being threatened inside the sanctuaries themselves by the growing demands for land and protein. It is unrealistic to contemplate any significant reduction in the growth rate of the human population of Africa before the turn of this century, and it would seem realistic to propose that if elephants are to survive in Africa they, and all other wildlife species, must be integrated into our land-use planning.

What then, for the future? I am firmly convinced that all conservation organisations must have the courage to adopt a long-term perspective and put pressure on governments whenever they can to tackle the broader issues involved in conservation planning. At present a great deal of time, energy, money and expertise is being devoted to minor issues, such as the translocation of locally endangered species, or the protection of a few hectares of an isolated woodland community, when the major issues are *still* unresolved and largely ignored.

There are three main areas in which positive remedial action is required: land-use planning, a reduction of the human population growth rate, and a reappraisal of the present system of conservation education. A completely new approach to *land-use planning* is paramount for it is a problem that requires immediate attention in the whole of Africa. As just one example, there is an urgent need to slow the accelerating downward spiral of land degradation associated with the unplanned settlement of people on land that is totally unsuited to primitive subsistence agriculture. All too often these people live next to national parks and wildlife reserves, and once their land has been degraded to the point of no return, they inevitably turn their attentions to the wildlife sanctuaries and demand to have this extra land. In short, unplanned subsistence agriculture is not sustainable, and is at best a short-term expediency.

Every African government appreciates that food production rates as a very high priority, and land with high agricultural potential will have to be used accordingly. Lands of low agricultural potential can then be assessed for other possible uses such as for exotic forests, cattle ranching, wildlife reserves or a host of multiple land-use purposes. Faced with these problems each country requires a positive rural land-use strategy which recognises the prime importance of food production, but at the same time safeguards soil, habitat and wildlife. Admittedly legitimate demands for the exploitation of mineral resources that are situated within wildlife sanctuaries need to be evaluated in terms of the national importance of the resource to the country concerned, but the broader long-term issues cannot be forgotten or overlooked. But if conservation organisations make

164

an out-of-hand rejection of such a demand for the exploitation of minerals, then they will be equally guilty of failing to maintain the very objectivity that is so essential in this new approach to *integrated* resource planning.

Purists might be alarmed by these concepts, for some existing wildlife sanctuaries would almost certainly face deproclamation. This must be accepted on one hand while on the other new sanctuaries must be created or expanded elsewhere on the basis of an objective land capability classification.

But before any comprehensive land-use planning can take place, each country must build up an adequate resource data base with readily available, up-to-date accurate information on all its natural resources stored in a form in which information is easily up-dated and retrievable. A Computerised Natural Resources Data Bank meets all these requirements, and would become an essential part of a new dynamic long-term approach to planning. Furthermore, such a system could be used to help identify as many as possible of the noteworthy areas of wildlife habitat, and to select from these areas representing nationally important examples. With this information available, conservation organisations could make realistic recommendations on how much habitat, and what patterns of distribution of fragmented habitats, are necessary to maintain ecosystems and populations.

Unfortunately, elephants are not compatible with agriculture and forestry and in the years to come they will be restricted to the larger wildlife sanctuaries, to controlled hunting areas or to smaller fenced areas such as the Addo Elephant Park in South Africa.

As unpalatable as it may appear, elephants will have to justify their existence by the money they earn from tourism, hunting and sustained-yield meat production – there is no realistic alternative.

Attempts to reorganise the distribution of people in relation to the optimum use of natural resources *must* be coupled with a sincere attempt to *reduce the human population growth rate*. Exponential growth of people and livestock and exponential consumption of natural resources cannot continue indefinitely in a finite world. Family planning on its own cannot bring about the desired result. India, the country which has spent the most money on family planning over the longest period of time, has in reality accomplished little. In 1951, when the family planning campaign was initiated, India's population grew by 3,6 million. In 1975 it grew by 16,2 million.

All African countries must come to appreciate the significance of these alarming statistics, and have the courage to overcome religious and political difficulties and put forward a declared *population policy* for each country that defines an optimum population size that will both conserve all natural resources and enhance the quality of the existence of the inhabitants.

Some slight progress is being made. In 1977 a decline in fertility had occurred in 77 of the 88 developing countries for which estimates were available. However, the fact remains that the current rate of decline in fertility in the developing countries is too slow to avoid their ultimately arriving at stationary populations far in excess of acceptable levels.

Robert McNamara, President of the World Bank, summed up the situation extremely well in an important speech on this subject in April 1977 when he said: 'Short of thermonuclear war itself, the problem of population growth is the gravest issue the world faces over the decades immediately ahead. Indeed, in many ways rampant population growth is an even more dangerous and subtle threat to the world than thermonuclear war, for it is intrinsically less subject to rational safeguards, and less amenable to organised control. Unless governments, through appropriate policy action, can accelerate the reduction in fertility, the global population may not stabilise below 11 000 000 000. That would be a world none of us would want to live in.'

Finally, fundamental changes are required in the field of *conservation education*. Throughout Africa there is a shocking lack of awareness of the environmental problems facing the continent, and this can only be rectified by schools and universities introducing compulsory courses on all aspects of conservation, including land-use planning, the ecological and economic value of wildlife right through to all relevant aspects of human ecology. Most important of all, decision-makers themselves must be made to appreciate that a realistic philosophy for conservation must be by its very nature related to human survival, and that conservation is not merely a remote academic subject.

The well-known ecologist, Ray Dasmann, summed it all up at the 12th General Assembly of the International Union for the Conservation of Nature and Natural Resources held in Zaïre in 1975 when he said: 'What we really need is conservation as if people mattered, and development as if nature mattered.'

At this point in time, perhaps as never before, there is a need for clarity of mind in defining the objectives and priorities for conservation in Africa. The elephant problem has come as a timely warning to us all – we cannot afford to ignore it.

Glossary

Adaptation: The process by which an organism becomes fitted to its environment.

Annual: A plant that completes its life cycle from seedling to mature seed-bearing plant in one season, and then dies.

Aorta: The great main artery which carries blood to the body through arteries and their branches.

Arteriosclerosis: A condition marked by loss of elasticity, thickening and hardening of the arteries.

Browser: An animal that feeds primarily on the leaves, buds and twigs of trees and shrubs.

Cardiovascular: Pertaining to the heart and blood vessels.

Carnivore: An animal that lives by eating the flesh of other animals.

Carrying capacity: The number of animals of a given size which can be supported for a given period of time by the vegetation growing in that area without adversely affecting the vegetation production.

Conception: The fertilisation of the ovum.

Cortex: The outer part of an organ.

Deciduous teeth: Teeth that are naturally shed during an animal's life.

Ecology: The science which deals with the relationship between plants and animals and their environment.

Ecosystem: The ecological system formed by the interaction of organisms and their environment.

Epididymis: A mass of tightly coiled tubes that lead spermatozoa away from the testis.

Fatty acids: A group of organic acids that occur in plants and animals.

Foetus: In the elephant, the unborn offspring in the uterus. Up to eight weeks of gestation it is called an embryo.

Grazer: An animal that feeds primarily on grass.

Habitat: The locality or living place of a plant or animal.

Herbivore: An animal that eats plants.

Homeostasis: A tendency to stability in the state of an organism or the numbers in a population.

Ilium: That part of the hip-bone supporting the flank.

Incisor: A premaxillary tooth of a mammal.

Indigenous: An animal or plant that is native to the locality.

Interstitial tissue: Tissue that occurs in the spaces between the main components of an organ.

Lesion: Damage or injury to an organ or tissue.

Linoleic acid: A fatty acid that occurs in various vegetable oils.

Lumbar depression: A depression in front of the ilium.

Luteal tissue: Tissue of the corpus luteum (see text for details).

Monovular: One ovulation at a time.

Neonatal: New-born.

Oocytes: The growing female reproductive cell that has not completed its process of maturation.

Ovary: The essential female reproductive gland.

Ovulation: The emission of eggs or ova from the ovary.

Ovum: The female reproductive cell prior to fertilisation.

Parasite: An organism living in or on another to its own advantage in terms of food and shelter.

Pathogen: Any disease-producing micro-organism.

Pelvic girdle: The 'girdle' of bones formed by the two hip-bones, sacrum and coccyx.

Perennial: Persisting through the year, or for a number of years.

Physiology: The science that deals with functions and activities of organisms.

Polyovular: Two or more ovulations at a time.

Premaxilla: A paired bone at the front of the skull in most vertebrates.

Pre-pubertal: A female that has not ovulated, or a male that has not produced spermatozoa.

Post-pubertal: A female that has ovulated at least once, or a male that has produced spermatozoa.

Riparian: Growing, or living on the banks of streams and rivers.

Savanna: Subtropical or tropical grassland with widely spaced trees.

Seminal vesicle: One of the accessory organs of reproduction in the male.

Shifting cultivation: A primitive farming method. By cutting and burning trees, a clearing is made in the woodland, where crops are planted for a few seasons until the soil loses its fertility. The plots are then abandoned, and the process starts again.

Spermatozoa: The male reproductive cells.

Territory: An area defended by an animal against others of the same species.

Testis: The essential male reproductive gland producing spermatozoa.

Testosterone: Male hormone produced by the testis.

References

The abbreviations used in the list of references follow the standard world list of abbreviations. The more common Journals are:

Anat.Rec.   Anatomical Record.

E.Afr.Wildl.J.   East African Wildlife Journal.

J.appl. Ecol.   Journal of Applied Ecology.

J.Mammal.   Journal of Mammalogy.

J.Physiol.Lond.   Journal of Physiology, London.

J.Reprod.Fert.   Journal of Reproduction and Fertility.

J.sth.Afr.Wild.Mgmt.Ass.   Journal of the Southern African Wildlife Management Association.

J.Wildl.Manage.   Journal of Wildlife Management.

J.Zool.,Lond.   Journal of Zoology, London.

Phil.Trans.R.Soc.B.   Philosophical Transactions of the Royal Society of London. Series B. Biological Sciences.

Proc.zool.Soc.Lond.   Proceedings of the Zoological Society of London.

CHAPTER 1

Brooks, A. C. & Buss, I. O. (1962). Past and present status of the elephant in Uganda. *J.Wildl.Manage.* 26(1): 38-50.

Grzimek, B. & M. (1960). *Serengeti shall not die.* Hamish Hamilton, London.

Hanks, J. (1967). The use of M.99 for the immobilisation of the Defassa waterbuck *(Kobus defassa penricei).* E.Afr. Wildl.J. 5: 96-105.

Tolba, M. K. (1977). The UN Conference on Desertification. *IUCN Bulletin.* 8(8/9): 43.

CHAPTER 2

Anderson, G. D. & Walker, B. H. (1974). Vegetation composition and elephant damage in the Sengwa Wildlife Research Area, Rhodesia. *J.sth.Afr.Wildl.Mgmt.Ass.* 4(1): 1-14.

Codrington, R. (1908). Exhibition of a collection of stones taken from the stomach of an elephant shot in N. Rhodesia. *Proc.zool.Soc.Lond.* 1908: 203.

Coe, M. (1972). Defaecation by African elephants *(Loxodonta africana africana* Blumenbach). *E.Afr.Wildl.J.* 10: 165-174.

Croze, H. (1974). The Seronera bull problem. I. The elephants. *E.Afr.Wildl.J.* 12: 1-27.

Croze, H. (1974). The Seronera bull problem. II. The trees. *E.Afr.Wildl.J.* 12: 29-47.

Darling, F. F. (1960). *Wild Life in an African Territory.* Oxford University Press: London.

Dodds, D. G. & Patton, D. R. (1968). *Wildlife and Land-use Survey of the Luangwa Valley.* FAO: Rome.

Game & Fisheries Annual Report (1964 & 1965). Ministry of Lands and Natural Resources, Government Printer, Lusaka.

Guy, P. (1974). *Feeding behaviour of the African elephant in the Sengwa Research Area of Rhodesia.* M.Sc. Thesis: University of Rhodesia.

Guy, P. (1975). The daily food intake of the African elephant, *Loxodonta africana* Blumenbach, in Rhodesia. *Arnoldia Rhod.* 7 (26): 1-8.

Hubbard, W. D. (1928). Observations on the elephants of Northern Rhodesia and Portuguese East Africa. *J.Mammal.* 9: 39-49.

Laws, R. M. (1970). Elephants as agents of habitat and landscape change in East Africa. *Oikos* 21: 1-15.

Lawton, R. M. (1966). *A survey of part of the Luangwa Valley, Zambia, to ascertain the causes of erosion and the relationship between erosion, vegetation type, game population and fire.* Mount Makulu Research Station: Chilanga, Zambia. Roneoed Report.

Lawton, R. M. (1970). Destruction or utilization of a wildlife habitat? In: *The Scientific Management of Animal and Plant Communities for Conservation.* Edits. E. Duffey & A. S. Watt. Blackwells: Oxford.

McCullagh, K. G. (1973). Are African Elephants Deficient in Essential Fatty Acids? *Nature* 242: 267-268.

Naylor, J. N., Caughley, G. J., Abel, N. D. J. & Liberg, O. (1973) *Luangwa Valley Conservation and Development Project. Zambia. Game Management and Habitat Manipulation.* FAO: Rome.

Offermann, P. P. M. (1953). The elephant in the Belgian Congo. In: *The Elephant in East Central Africa.* Rowland Ward: London.

Pitman, C. R. S. (1934). *A report on a faunal survey of Northern Rhodesia.* Government Printer: Livingstone.

Thomson, P. J. (1975). The role of elephants, fire and other agents in the decline of a *Brachystegia boehmii* woodland. *J.sth.Afr. Wildl.Mgmt.Ass.* 5(1): 11-18.

Verboom, W. C. (1968). *Report on the visit to the vegetation plots laid down by Mr W. L. Astle in the Luangwa South Game Reserve.* Dept. of Agriculture: Lusaka. Roneoed Report.

Western, D. (1973). The changing face of Amboseli. *Africana* 5(3): 23-27.

Wyatt, J. R. & Eltringham, S. K. (1974). The daily activity of the elephant in the Rwenzori National Park, Uganda. *E.Afr.Wildl.J.* 12:273-289.

CHAPTER 3

Game and Fisheries Annual Report (1965). Ministry of Lands & Natural Resources, Government Printer, Lusaka.

Hanks, J. (1969). The capture of young elephant in the Zambezi valley. *Puku* 5: 87-90.

Hanks, J. (1971). *The reproductive physiology of the African elephant, Loxodonta africana.* Ph.D. Thesis, University of Cambridge.

Steel, W. S. (1968). The technology of wildlife management game cropping in the Luangwa Valley, Zambia. *E.Afr.agric.For.J.* 33:266-270.

CHAPTER 4

Brownlee, J. W. & Hanks, J. (1977). Notes on the growth of young male African elephants. *Lammergeyer* 23: 7-12.

Brown, C. E. (1934). Captive pygmy elephants in America. *J.Mammal.* 15: 248-250.

Croze, H. (1972). A modified photogrammetric technique for assessing age-structure of elephant populations and its use in Kidepo National Park. *E.Afr.Wildl.J.* 10: 91-115.

Elder, W. H. (1970). Morphometry of elephant tusks. *Zoologica Africana.* 5(1): 143-159.

Hanks, J. (1972). Growth of the African elephant *(Loxodonta africana). E.Afr.Wildl.J.* 10:251-272.

Hanks, J. (1972). Aspects of dentition of the African elephant, *Loxodonta africana. Arnoldia Rhod.* 5(36): 1-8.

Hanks, J. (1972). Reproduction of the elephant *(Loxodonta africana)* in the Luangwa Valley, Zambia. *J.Reprod.Fert.* 30: 13-26.

Johnson, O. W. & Buss, I. O. (1965). Molariform teeth of male African elephants in relation to age, body dimensions, and growth. *J.Mammal.* 46(3): 373-384.

Krumrey, W. A. & Buss, I. O. (1968). Age estimation, growth and relationships between body dimensions of the female African elephant. *J.Mammal.* 49(1): 22-31.

Laws. R. M. (1966). Age criteria for the African elephant, *Loxodonta africana. E.Afr. Wildl.J.* 4: 1-37.

Laws, R. M. (1967). Eye lens weight and age in African elephants. *E.Afr.Wildl.J.* 5: 46-52.

Laws, R. M. (1969). Aspects of reproduction in the African elephant, *Loxodonta africana. J.Reprod.Fert.Suppl.* 6: 193-217.

Laws, R. M. (1969). Tsavo Research Project. *J.Reprod.Fert.Suppl.* 6: 495-531.

Laws, R. M. & Parker, I.S.C. (1968). Recent studies on elephant populations in East Africa. *Symp.zool.Soc.Lond.* 21: 319-359.

Laws, R. M., Parker, I. S. C. & Archer, A. L. (1967). Estimating live weights of elephants from hind leg weight. *E.Afr.Wildl.J.* 5: 106-111.

Laws, R. M., Parker, I.S.C. & Johnstone, R. C. B. (1970). Elephants and habitats in North Bunyoro, Uganda. *E.Afr.Wildl.J.* 8: 163-180.

Pocock, R. I. (1918). The ages of elephants, as inferred from the molar teeth. *Proc.zool.Soc.Lond.* 1918: 303.

Short, R. V. (1969). Notes on the teeth and ovaries of an African elephant *(Loxodonta africana)* of known age. *J.Zool.Lond.,* 158: 421-425.

Sikes, S. K. (1966). The African elephant, *Loxodonta africana*: a field method for the estimation of age. *J.Zool.Lond.*, 150: 279-295.

Sikes, S. K. (1968). The African elephant, *Loxodonta africana*: a field method for the estimation of age. *J.Zool.Lond.*, 154:235-248.

Smuts, G. L. (1975). Reproduction and population characteristics of elephants in the Kruger National Park. *J.sth.Afr.Wildl.Mgmt.Ass.* 5(1): 1-10.

Spinage, C. A. (1959). An apparent case of precocious tusk growth in a young African elephant. *Proc.zool.Soc.Lond.* 133(1): 45.

CHAPTER 5

Buss, I. O. & Johnson, O. W. (1967). Relationships of Leydig cell characteristics and intratesticular testosterone levels to sexual activity in the African elephant. *Anat.Rec.* 157(2): 191-196.

Buss, I. O. & Savidge, J. M. (1966). Change in population number and reproductive rate of elephants in Uganda. *J.Wildl.Manage.* 30(4): 791-809.

Darling, F. F. (1960). *Wild Life in an African Territory.* Oxford University Press: London.

Hanks, J. (1969). Seasonal breeding of the African elephant in Zambia. *E.Afr.Wildl.J.* 7: 167.

Hanks, J. (1972). Reproduction of the elephant *(Loxodonta africana)* in the Luangwa Valley, Zambia. *J.Reprod.Fert.* 30: 13-25.

Hanks, J. (1973). Growth and development of the ovary of the African elephant, *Loxodonta africana* Blumenbach. *Puku* 7: 125-131.

Hanks, J. (1973). Reproduction in the male African elephant in the Luangwa Valley, Zambia. *J.sth.Afr.Wildl.Mgmt.Assoc.* 3(2): 31-39.

Hanks, J. (1977). Comparative aspects of reproduction in the male hyrax and elephant. In: *Reproduction and Evolution.* Edits. J. H. Calaby and C. H. Tyndale-Biscoe: 155-164. Australian Academy of Science, Canberra.

Hanks, J. & Short, R. V. (1972). The formation and function of the corpus luteum of the African elephant *(Loxodonta africana).* *J.Reprod.Fert.* 29: 79-89.

Huggett, A. St. G. & Widdas, W. F. (1951). The relationship between mammalian foetal weight and conception age. *J.Physiol.Lond.* 114: 306-317.

Jainudeen, M. R., Katongole, C. B. & Short, R. V. (1972). Plasma testosterone levels in relation to musth and sexual activity in the male Asiatic elephant *Elephas maximus. J.Reprod.Fert.* 29: 99-103.

Jainudeen, M. R., McKay, G. M. & Eisenberg, J. F. (1972). Observations on musth in the domesticated Asiatic elephant. *Mammalia* 36(2): 247-261.

Jones, E. C. (1970). The ageing ovary and its influence on reproductive capacity. *J.Reprod.Fert.Suppl.* 12: 17-30.

Jones, R. C., Rowlands, I. W. & Skinner, J. D. (1974). Spermatozoa in the genital ducts of the African elephant, *Loxodonta africana. J.Reprod.Fert.* 41: 189-192.

Lang, E. M. (1967). The birth of an African elephant at Basle Zoo. *Int.ZooYb.* VII: 154-157.

Laws, R. M. (1967). Occurrence of placental scars in the uterus of the African elephant *(Loxodonta africana).* *J.Reprod.Fert.* 14: 445-449.

Laws, R. M. (1969). Aspects of reproduction in the African elephant, *Loxodonta africana. J.Reprod.Fert.Suppl.* 6: 193-217.

Laws, R. M. & Parker, I. S. C. (1968). Recent studies on elephant populations in East Africa. *Symp.zool.Soc.Lond.* 21: 319-359.

Laws, R. M., Parker, I. S. C. & Johnstone, R. C. B. (1970). Elephants and habitats in North Bunyoro, Uganda. *E.Afr.Wildl.J.* 8: 163-180.

Leuthold, W. & Leuthold, B. M. (1975). Parturition and related behaviour in the African elephant. *Z.Tierpsychol.* 39: 75-84.

Lyne, A. G. (1974). Gestation period and birth in the Marsupial, *Isoodon macrourus. Aust.J.Zool.* 22: 303-309.

Perry, J. S. (1953). The reproduction of the African elephant, *(Loxodonta africana).* *Phil.Trans.R.Soc.B.* 237: 93-149.

Perry, J. S. (1964). The structure and development of the reproductive organs of the female African elephant. *Phil.trans.R.Soc.B.* 248: 35-51.

Perry, J. S. (1974). Implantation, foetal membranes and early placentation of the African elephant, *Loxodonta africana. Phil.Trans.R.Soc.B.* 269: 109-135.

Plotka, E. D., Seal, U. S., Schobert, E. E. & Schmoller, G. C. (1975). Serum progesterone and estrogens in elephants. *Endocrinology* 97: 485-487.

Roth, H. H. (1963). Abnormale Laktation eines afrikanischen Elefanten. *D.Zool.Gart.Leipzig.* 26: 122-123.

Seth-Smith, A. M. D. & Parker, I. S. C. (1967). A record of twin foetuses in the African elephant. *E.Afr.Wildl.J.* 5: 167.

Short, R. V. (1966). Oestrous behaviour, ovulation and the formation of the corpus luteum in the African elephant, *Loxodonta africana. E.Afr.Wildl.J.* 4:56-68.

Short, R. V. (1972). Species differences. In: *Reproduction in Mammals. 5. Reproductive Patterns.* Edits. C. R. Austin and R. V. Short. University Press: Cambridge.

Short, R. V., Mann, T., & Hay, M. F. (1967). Male reproductive organs of the African elephant, *Loxodonta africana. J.Reprod.Fert.* 13: 517-536.

Simpson, G. G. (1954). The principles of classification and a classification of mammals. *Bull.Amer.Mus.Nat.Hist.* 85.pp. 1-350.

Smith, J. A. & Ross, W. D. (eds.) (1910). *Historia Animalium. The works of Aristotle.* Vol. IV. Clarendon Press: Oxford.

Smith, J. G., Hanks, J. & Short, R. V. (1969). Biochemical observations on the corpora lutea of the African elephant, *Loxodonta africana. J.Reprod.Fert.* 20: 111-117.

Smuts, G. C. (1975). Reproduction and population characteristics of elephants in the Kruger National Park. *J.sth.Afr.Wildl.Mgmt.Ass.* 5(1): 1-10.

CHAPTER 6

Bere, R. M. (1966). *The African elephant.* A. Barker: London.

Burton, J. A. (1977). Kenya's wildlife ban. *New Scientist.* 74(1053): 442.

Burton, J. A. (1977). The ivory connection, part 2. *New Scientist.* 76(1074): 168-169.

Buss, I. O. & Brooks, A. C. (1961). Observations on number, mortality and reproduction of elephants in Uganda. *CCTA/IUCN Symposium: Arusha.*

Bourlière. F. & Verschuren, J. (1960). Introduction à l'écologie des ongulés du Parc National Albert. *Explor.Parc natn.Albert Miss. F. Bourlière J. Verschuren.* 1: 1-158.

Carr, N. J. (1950). Elephants in the Eastern Province. *Nth.Rhod.J.* 2: 25-28.

Condy, J. B. (1974). Observations on internal parasites in Rhodesian elephant, *Loxodonta africana* Blumenbach 1797. *Proc.&Trans.Rhod.Sci.Assoc.* 55(2): 67-99.

Corfield. T. F. (1973). Elephant mortality in Tsavo National Park, Kenya. *E.Afr.Wildl.J.* 11: 339-368.

Davison, T. (1967). *Wankie, the story of a great Game Reserve.* Books of Africa: Cape Town.

Dillman, J. S. & Carr, W. R. (1970). Observations on arteriosclerosis, serum cholesterol and serum electrolytes in the wild African elephant *(Loxodonta africana). J.comp.Path.* 80: 81-87.

Douglas-Hamilton, I. (1973). On the ecology and behaviour of the Lake Manyara elephants. *E.Afr.Wildl.J.* 11: 401-403.

Eltringham, S. K. & Malpas, R. C. (1976). Elephant slaughter in Uganda. *Oryx* 13: 334-335.

Hanks, J. (1971). *The reproductive physiology of the African elephant, Loxodonta africana.* Ph.D. Thesis, Univ. of Cambridge.

Holman, D. (1967). *The elephant people.* Murray: London.

Johnston, H. H. (1897). *British Central Africa.* Methuen: London.

Krumrey, W. A. & Buss, I. O. (1969). Observations on the adrenal gland of the African elephant. *J.Mammal.* 50(1): 90-101.

Laws, R. M. (1966). Age criteria for the African elephant, *Loxodonta africana. E.Afr.Wildl.J.* 4:1-37.

Laws, R. M. (1969). Tsavo Research Project. *J.Reprod.Fert.Suppl.* 6: 495-531.

Laws, R. M. & Parker, I. S. C. (1968). Recent studies on elephant populations in East Africa. *Symp.zool.Soc.Lond.* 21: 319-359.

Malpas. R. C. (1977). Diet and the condition and growth of elephants in Uganda. *J.appl.Ecol.* 14: 489-504.

McCullagh, K. G. (1972). Arteriosclerosis in the African elephant. Prt.I.Intimal Atherosclerosis and its possible causes. *Atheroschlerosis* 16: 307-335.

McCullagh, K. G. & Lewis, M. C. (1967). Spontaneous arteriosclerosis in the wild African elephant; its relation to disease in man. *Lancet* ii: 492-495.

172

Melland, F. (1938). *Elephants in Africa*. Country Life: London.

Morris, R. C. (1927). On 'natural deaths' in wild elephants. *J.Bombay nat.Hist.Soc.* 32: 794-795.

Offermann, P. P. M. (1953). The elephant in the Belgian Congo. In: *The Elephant in East Central Africa*. Rowland Ward: London.

Pienaar, U. de V. (1969). Predator-prey relationship amongst the larger mammals of the Kruger National Park. *Koedoe* 12: 108-176.

Pienaar, U. de V., Wyk, P. van & Fairall, N. (1966). An aerial census of elephant and buffalo in the Kruger National Park and the implications thereof on intended management schemes. *Koedoe* 9: 40-107.

Pitman. C. R. S. (1945). *A game warden takes stock*. Nisbet: London.

Sikes, S. K. (1969). Habitat and cardiovascular disease: observations made on elephants (*Loxodonta africana*) and other free-living animals in East Africa. *Trans.zool.Soc.Lond.* (1969) 32: 1-104.

Sikes, S. K. (1971). *The natural history of the African elephant*. Weidenfeld & Nicolson: London.

Springe, C. A. (1973). A review of ivory exploitation and elephant population trends in Africa. *E.Afr.Wildl.J.* 11: 281-289.

Tinker, J. (1975). Who's killing Kenya's jumbos? *New Scientist*. 66(950): 452-455.

Trimmer, C. D. (1962). Uganda National Parks Report for the Quarter ending 31 Dec. 1962. (mimeo).

Williamson, B. R. (1975). Seasonal distribution of elephant in Wankie National Park. *Arnoldia Rhod.* 7(11): 1-16.

CHAPTER 7

Caughley, G. & Goddard, J. (1975). Abundance and distribution of elephants in the Luangwa Valley, Zambia. *E.Afr.Wildl.J.* 13: 39-48.

Croze, H. (1974). The Seronera bull problem. 1. The elephants. *E.Afr.Wildl.J.* 12: 1-27.

Douglas-Hamilton, I. (1973). On the ecology and behaviour of the Lake Manyara elephants. *E.Afr.Wildl.J.* 11: 401-403.

Douglas-Hamilton, I. & O. (1975). *Among the elephants*. Collins & Harvill Press: London.

Hanks, J. (1969). Techniques for marking large African mammals. *Puku* 5: 65-86.

Henshaw, J. (1972). Notes on conflict between elephants and some bovids and on other specific contacts in Yankari Game Reserve, N. E. Nigeria. *E.Afr.Wildl.J.* 10: 151-153.

Johnston, H. H. (1897). *British Central Africa*. Methuen: London.

Kerr, M. A. & Frazer, J. A. (1975). Distribution of elephant in a part of the Zambezi Valley, Rhodesia. *Arnoldia Rhod.* 7(21): 1-14.

Laws, R. M. (1969). Tsavo Research Project. *J.Reprod.Fert.Suppl.* 6. 495-531.

Leuthold, W. & Sale, J. B. (1973). Movements and patterns of habitat utilization of elephants in Tsavo National Park, Kenya. *E.Afr.Wildl.J.* 11: 369-384.

Naylor, J. N., Caughley, G. J., Abel, N. D. J. & Liberg, O. (1973). *Luangwa Valley Conservation and Development Project. Zambia. Game Management and Habitat Manipulation*. FAO: Rome.

Pitman, C. R. S. (1934). *A report on a faunal survey of Northern Rhodesia*. Government Printer: Livingstone.

Pocock, R. I. (1916). Scent-glands in mammals. *Proc.zool.Soc.Lond.* 1916: 742-755.

Poles, W. E. (1951). *Game Population and distribution in the Luangwa Valley within the Mpika District in the year 1951*. Dept. of Game and Tsetse Control: Chilanga. Roneoed Report.

Sharp, A. (1904). Game Census of the British Central African Protectorate. *J.Soc.Preserv.Fauna Emp.* Pt. 1: 73-74.

Uys, J. M. C (1964). *A report on the results of an aerial game population survey*. Dept. of Game & Fisheries: Fort Jameson. Roneoed Report.

Weir, J. S. (1972). Spatial distribution of elephants in an African National Park in relation to environmental sodium. *Oikos* 23: 1-13.

Weir, J. S. (1972). Mineral content of elephant dung. *E.Afr.Wildl.J.* 10: 229-230.

Weir, J. S. (1973). Exploitation of water soluble soil sodium by elephants in Murchison Falls National Park, Uganda. *E.Afr.Wildl.J.* 11: 1-7.

WWF/IUCN. (1976/77). *Elephant Survey and Conservation Programme*. Newsletters 1 & 2. WWF, Nairobi.

Wyatt, J. R. & Eltringham, S. K. (1974). The daily activity of the elephant in the Rwenzori National Park, Uganda. *E.Afr.Wildl.J.* 12: 273-289.

173

CHAPTER 8

Anon. (1973). *KwaZulu Annual Report.* Department of Agriculture and Forestry: Pietermaritzburg.

Blackwelder, J. (1975). The real crises behind the 'Food Crisis'. *Environmental Conservation* 2(2): 131.

Butynski, T. M. & Von Richter, W. (1975). Wildlife Management in Botswana. *Wildlife Society Bulletin* 3(1): 19-24.

Caughley, G. (1976). The elephant problem – an alternative hypothesis. *E.Afr.Wildl.J.* 14: 265-283.

Douglas-Hamilton, I. (1973). On the ecology and behaviour of the Lake Manyara elephants. *E.Afr.Wildl.J.* 11: 401-403.

Eberhardt, L. L. (1977). Optimal policies for conservation of large mammals, with special reference to marine ecosystems. *Environmental conservation* 4(3): 205-212.

Ehrlich, P. R. & Holdren, J. P. (1975). Eight thousand million people by the year 2010? *Environmental Conservation* 2(4): 241-242.

Fowler, C. W. & Smith, T. (1973). Characterizing stable population: an application to the African elephant population. *J.Wildl.Manage.* 37(4): 513-523.

Grice, D. C. (1973). *The approaching crisis – land and population in the Transvaal and Natal.* Presidential Address to the S.A. Institute of Race Relations, January, 1973.

Hanks, J. (1973). The population explosion in Rhodesia and the consequence of unlimited growth. *Rhodesia Science News.* 7(9): 249-256.

Hanks, J. (1974). The human population explosion – is there a global solution? *Rhodesia Science News* 8(8): 245-253.

Hanks, J. (1975). Population growth and environmental awareness in relation to ecosystem management. *Rhodesia Science News* 9(1): 4-6.

Hanks, J. (1975). Population problems of Rhodesia. *Rhodesia Science News* 9(6): 172-174.

Hanks, J. (1976). Will Wildlife Survive? *African Wildlife* 30(4): 29-32.

Hanks, J. & McIntosh, J. E. A. (1973). Population dynamics of the African elephant *(Loxodonta africana). J.Zool.,Lond.* 169:29-38.

Huxley, J. (1961). *The conservation of wildlife and natural habitats in Central and East Africa.* Unesco: Paris.

Lamprey, H. F. (1963). Ecological separation of the large mammals species in the Tarangire Game Reserve, Tanganyika. *E.Afr.Wildl.J.* 1: 63-92.

Laws, R. M., Parker, I.S.C. & Johnstone, R. C. B. (1975). *Elephants and their habitats. The ecology of elephants in North Bunyoro, Uganda.* Clarendon Press, Oxford.

Malthus, T. R. (1798). "*An essay on the principle of population, as it affects the future improvement of society.*" Printed for J. Johnson in St. Paul's Churchyard, London.

Naylor, J. N., Caughley, G. J., Abel, N. D. J. & Liberg, O. (1973). *Luangwa Valley Conservation and Development Project. Zambia. Game Management and Habitat Manipulation.* FAO: Rome.

Nortman, D. & Hofstatter, E. (1975). Population and family planning programs: a factbook. *Reports on Population/Family Planning.* 2 (7th edition): 1-86.

Sheldrick, D. (1972). Tsavo. The hard lessons of history. *Africana* 4(10): 14-15; 26-28.

Vincent, V. & Thomas, R. G. (1960). *An agricultural survey of Southern Rhodesia: Part 1: Agro-ecological survey.* Government Printer: Salisbury.

Walker, B. R. (1977). South Africa needs an Institute of Natural Resources. *African Wildlife.* 31(2): 37.

Index

References to illustrations are in italic

175

176